PSYCHOLOGY
AND
THE HUMAN DILEMMA

by

ROLLO MAY

D. VAN NOSTRAND COMPANY

NEW YORK   CINCINNATI   TORONTO   LONDON   MELBOURNE

D. VAN NOSTRAND COMPANY REGIONAL OFFICES:
New York   Cincinnati   Millbrae

D. VAN NOSTRAND COMPANY INTERNATIONAL OFFICES:
London   Toronto   Melbourne

Library of Congress Catalog Card Number 66-30544
ISBN: 0-442-05186-7

Published by D. VAN NOSTRAND COMPANY
450 West 33rd Street, New York, N. Y. 10001

Published simultaneously in Canada by
VAN NOSTRAND REINHOLD LTD.

10   9   8   7   6

FOREWORD

These essays, most of which were written in the past four years, have a common theme. It arises out of the great variety, richness, and span of human experience—a vast spectrum shown, for example, by man's capacity for admirable reason on one hand and the far reach of his irrational behavior on the other, the joy and productivity of which he is capable and his ever-present proclivity for despair and self-defeat. The very extent and range of this spectrum, I propose, introduces certain distinguishing characteristics into human consciousness, some of which we shall discuss in this book under the term "dilemma." It has long been my conviction that man's total experience, as shown in such polarities, is part of the subject matter of psychology and must be taken into account if that discipline is to merit the title of "a science of man." I hope these essays will make some contribution to that end.

The word "dilemma" is not used here in its technical sense. I do not mean an insoluble problem, as is implied in the phrase "two horns of a dilemma," one horn of which is bound to impale you if the other does not. I use it rather as referring to polarity or paradox. To be sure, the dilemmas can result in stalemate, blockage, anxious over-development of one side to escape the other. Hence the many disturbances and problems which bring people to our psychotherapeutic clinics and consulting offices. But this polarity is also the source of dynamic and human creativity. I believe that it is out of the constructive confronting of the tensions in these paradoxes that man builds cultures and civilizations.

A NOTE ON THE CHAPTERS OF THE PRESENT VOLUME

Some of the chapters of this book represent in modified form papers and lectures that have been published elsewhere, as follows:

Parts of Chapter 2 are from a lecture entitled "Modern Man's Image of Himself," delivered as one of the Alden Tuthill Lectures at Chicago Theological Seminary, University of Chicago, February 1962.

Chapter 3 draws on a lecture delivered under the title "Anxiety Among Students and Its Relation to Education" at the annual convention of the New England Association of Colleges and Secondary Schools, Boston, December 1964, and published in the *New England Association Review*.

Parts of Chapter 4 are based on a paper delivered at the Annual Convention of the American Psychopathological Association, and published in their volume, *Anxiety,* Hock and Zubin, eds., Grune and Stratton, 1951.

Chapter 5 draws on a lecture delivered at the annual convention of the American Psychiatric Association in 1956 and published in *Progress in Psychotherapy,* Grune and Stratton, New York, 1957.

Chapter 6 was delivered as a lecture at the Graduate Psychology Department of the University of Chicago and published in *Contemporary Psychotherapies,* edited by Morris I. Stein, Free Press, Glencoe, Ill., 1961.

Chapter 7 is based on a lecture delivered at the First Annual Conference on Phenomenology and Psychiatry, Veterans Hospital, Lexington, Ky., and published in *Phenomenology Pure and Applied,* edited by Erwin Straus, Duquesne University Press, Pittsburgh, 1965.

In an earlier form Chapter 8 was delivered at the Third International Congress on Psychotherapy at Barcelona in 1959 and published in *Topical Problems of Psychotherapy,* S. Karger, Basel and New York, 1960, Vol. 3.

Chapter 9 in its original form was an introduction to the paperback edition of Jean-Paul Sartre's *Existential Psychoanalysis,* Chicago, Regnéry, 1963.

Chapter 10 in its original form was published in the *Review of Existential Psychology and Psychiatry,* Vol. 3, No. 1, Winter 1963, pp. 5-10.

The original of Chapter 11 appeared in *Psychiatry: Journal for the Study of Interpersonal Relations,* Vol. 15, No. 4, November 1952. Part also appeared in my book *Man's Search for Himself,* Norton, New York, 1963.

Chapter 12 in its original form appeared in *Behavioral Science and Guidance: Proposals and Perspectives,* edited by Lloyd-Jones and Westervelt, Bureau of Publications, Teachers College, Columbia University, 1963.

The original of Chapter 13 was an address on the occasion of the Annual Award of the New York Society of Clinical Psychologists at the New York Academy of Sciences, 1955.

The original of Chapter 14 was a paper delivered in a symposium on Social Responsibilities of the Psychologist at the annual convention of the American Psychological Association in September 1963.

CONTENTS

. . . Lycon says in the trial [of Socrates]—"No faith will bear examination, a tree cannot live if you look at its roots."

Yet freedom can live only when life is constantly examined and where there are no censors to tell men how far their investigations can go. Human life lives in this paradox and on the horns of this dilemma. Examination is life, and examination is death. It is both, and it is the tension between.

—Maxwell Anderson, *"Notes on Socrates," Drama Section,* New York Times, *October 28, 1951*

1

Introduction: What Is the Human Dilemma?

> However, one should not think slightingly of the
> paradoxical; the paradox is the source of the thinker's
> passion, and the thinker without paradox is like a lover
> without feeling: a paltry mediocrity.
>
> —KIERKEGAARD, Fragments, p. 29

Once in a while I catch myself having a curious phantasy. It goes
something like this.

A psychologist—any psychologist, or all of us—arrives at the heav-
enly gates at the end of his long and productive life. He is brought
up before St. Peter for the customary accounting. Formidable, St.
Peter sits calmly behind his table looking like the Moses of Michel-
angelo. An angel assistant in a white jacket drops a manila folder on
the table which St. Peter opens and looks at, frowning. Despite the
awesome visage of the judge, the psychologist clutches his briefcase
and steps up with commendable courage.

But St. Peter's frown deepens. He drums with his fingers on the
table and grunts a few nondirective "uhm-uhm"s as he fixes the
candidate with his Mosaic eyes.

The silence is discomfiting. Finally the psychologist opens his briefcase and cries, "Here! The reprints of my hundred and thirty-two
papers."

St. Peter slowly shakes his head.

Burrowing deeper into the briefcase the psychologist offers, "Let
me submit the medals I received for my scientific achievement."

3

St. Peter's frown is unabated as he silently continues to stare into the psychologist's face.

At last St. Peter speaks. "I'm aware, my good man, how industrious you were. It's not sloth you're accused of. Nor is it unscientific behavior." Falling into silence again, his brow becomes darker. The psychologist realizes that long before confession was taken over on the analyst's couch, it was rated fairly highly at this very gate.

"Well, it's true," he admits with a fine show of frankness, "I did twist the data a bit on my Ph.D. research."

But St. Peter will not be placated. "No," he says, taking up Form 1-A from the dossier, "it's not immorality that's down on this document. You're as ethical as the next man. Nor am I accusing you of being a behaviorist or a mystic or a functionalist or an existentialist or a Rogerian. Those are only minor sins."

Now St. Peter slaps his hand resoundingly down on the table, and his tone is like Moses breaking the news of the ten commandments: "You are charged with *nimis simplicando!*

"You have spent your life making molehills out of mountains—that's what you're guilty of. When man was tragic, you made him trivial. When he was picaresque, you called him picayune. When he suffered passively, you described him as simpering; and when he drummed up enough courage to act, you called it stimulus and response. Man had passion; and when you were pompous and lecturing to your class you called it 'the satisfaction of basic needs,' and when you were relaxed and looking at your secretary you called it 'release of tension.' You made man over into the image of your childhood Erector Set or Sunday School maxims—both equally horrendous.

"In short, we sent you to earth for seventy-two years to a Dantean circus, and you spent your days and nights at sideshows! Nimis simplicando! * What do you plead, guilty or not guilty?"

"Oh, guilty, your celestial honor," stammers the psychologist. "Or rather I mean not guilty. For I was trying to study man as he behaves —isn't that what psychology is for? And your own Good Book says

* Latin scholars tell me *nimis* means "excessive," and *simplicandum* "simplifying." Or in our modern vernacular, *oversimplifying.*

that man is a worm, and 'there is no health in him.' So wasn't I discharging the task expected of me?'"

St. Peter brushes Form 1-A off the table with his forearm and leans over into the psychologist's face. "You didn't even *see* the man you were studying! Don't you think *I* know he's a worm at times? But that worm also stands upright and lays stone on stone to make the Parthenon. And that man paused one night on the desert beside the Nile and gazed up at the stars and wondered. And when the stars were setting he went back to his cave hut in the hillside and studied the ibis legs painted on his pottery. And he seized a charred stick from his fire and drew a triangle on the wall, and he made mathematics. And so he taught himself to tell the orbits of the stars, and learned to plant his crops by the rising and falling of the Nile. *A worm do that?* All that you forgot, didn't you?"

The psychologist steps back. "Your honor, I only tried to let man speak for himself!"

"Oh, you did, did you? What about all those experiments?" St. Peter gestures toward the still open briefcase. "I read your papers by celestial microfilm last night when we heard you were coming. What about all those experiments in which the punch line consists of lying to your man? 'Press this lever, it gives pain to the fellow on the other side of the window.' And you set up the man who was the decoy to grimace and play the game. 'Which line is the longer? Class?' 'Oh, the shorter is the longer.' 'And you, Mr. Fall-guy-subject, do you still stupidly contend against the whole class that the longer line is the longer?' "

St. Peter sighs and settles back. "I confess that's the one thing I never could understand about you fellows. Once you get your Ph.D.'s. you assume you can fool other human beings all the time. You couldn't fool your dog that way—he'd see through the pretense immediately."

The psychologist's attempted defense, "But the subjects all willingly participated in the experiment . . ." is drowned out by St. Peter's stentorian tones, "Oh, don't think I don't know that—the human animal has a great capacity to pretend he's fooled, and not even to let himself know he's pretending. But it's *you* I had thought better of—" and he levels a long bony finger at the psychologist. "*You* thought everybody could be fooled. Everybody but you. You always assumed that you, the fooler, were never fooled! Not a very consistent theory, is it?"

St. Peter sighs. The psychologist opens his mouth, but St. Peter raises his hand. "Please! Not your well-practiced chatter. Something new is required . . . something new." He sits back, meditating. . . .

And about that time I find myself meditating too. The phantasy has many endings—as many as your mood at the given moment. But whatever the ending, and however each of us may fare on the celestial entrance examination, must we not ask whether St. Peter has not, as the expression goes, got something?

This book thus begins on a note of irreverence. And I fear I must warn the reader that the present chapter, at least, will continue that way. For have we not in psychology overlooked, if not outright suppressed much of the time, considerations in human experience of basic importance? I propose to cite some of these considerations occurring to me which cluster around what I shall call here the "human dilemma."

What is the human dilemma? Let me illustrate it in its most elemental form; and though I shall be simplifying, I hope I shall not be guilty of *nimis simplicandum*.

I sit here at my typewriter of a morning writing on one of the chapters which follow in this book. As I work I experience myself as a man who has to get a chapter done, who has set himself a deadline, who has patients coming this afternoon whom he must be prepared to see beginning at two o'clock, and who must take some medicine to ward off a threatening cold. I glance up at the clock and I quickly count through the number of pages I have completed so far. As I write I find the uncomfortable thought pressing in, "My colleague, Professor So-and-So, will not like this point; perhaps I should obfuscate my idea a little—make it sound profound and not so easy to attack?" I nobly ward off such an ignoble temptation; but I do shore up the defenses of my argument, then pull myself away from the intruding thoughts and back to my typewriter.

Now in the state I have just described, I am viewing and treating myself as an object, a man to be controlled and directed in order to perform most effectively the task at hand. Note that my sentences hinge on such verbs as *have to, must, set* a deadline. And my questions to myself are some variation of, What is the best way to get this done? the most effective technique? *Time is external, set by the calendar and clock.* I treat myself as one who must "fit in"; I am gratified at that moment that I am a creature of habit without much leeway in behavior; and my aim is to make this leeway even less, to control my behavior more rigidly so that my chapter will be finished most expeditiously.

But as I continue writing I find myself suddenly caught up in an interesting idea. Ah, here is something that has been playing around the fringes of my consciousness for years—what an alluring prospect to work it out now, form it, see where it leads! I look out of the window a moment, musing, then write on, quite unaware of the passage of time. I find myself thinking, "Great! This idea makes sense of the whole argument—I want to put it here, I'll rearrange my whole chapter so." And I experience an exhilarating feeling of this-will-be-of-value—it's worth somebody's reading. Now when I catch myself thinking, "Colleague So-and-So won't like this," I scarcely pause to answer, 'The hell with him—if he doesn't it's his own hard luck, I want to write it anyway.' I type on, and suddenly, in what seems only a few minutes later, I become aware that it is twelve-thirty, half an hour past the time I had planned to stop

In this second state—the description of which undoubtedly reveals my own bias—I am viewing myself not as object but as subject. My sentences now hinge on such verbs as *want, wish, feel*, rather than *have* and *must*. In the first state I was the object of time; in this second, I am the subject of it. I am no longer the "slave of time," but neither are the clock and calendar completely irrelevant. *Time is open before me to use as I choose.* In the first I have put myself in a deterministic state; in the second the accent is on my leeway, my margin of freedom to choose and mold my behavior as I go along. The goal of the first state is efficient behavior, the significance of what I do being mostly *extrinsic* to my actions. The accent in the second state is the experiencing and choosing of things of *intrinsic* significance. Again, the verbs are illustrative: in the first state, *have to, must, set* are related to behavior in the service of an *external value,* which I have at least partially accepted, getting the chapter done. In the second, the *wanting, wishing, feeling* are verbs which have to do with the inner *act of valuing.*

X *The human dilemma is that which arises out of a man's capacity to experience himself as both subject and object at the same time.* Both are necessary—for the science of psychology, for therapy, and for gratifying living.

This dilemma can be illustrated at every moment in psychotherapy. I can view my patient in terms of diagnostic categories, an organism who fits to a greater or lesser extent such and such a pattern. I know, for example, that frequent urination is often connected with competitive patterns in the individual in our culture. This approach takes the patient as objective, and it is entirely legitimate from one side. But I cannot at that moment identify with the patient, experience what he is experiencing. Strictly speaking, to the extent I see him as an object, I cannot understand his sentences when he speaks. Some capacity to participate in subjective empathy is required even to understand another's language, as I shall show in a later chapter in this book. (Hence it is so difficult, almost impossible, to understand someone we hate.) When consulting with a borderline patient, for another example, I must consider whether he needs hospitalization and in such case what is the best method, and so on; but at that moment I am standing outside him and not doing therapy. If I am to do therapy with him I must not be preoccupied with how bizarre and meaningless are his utterances, but what is the hidden meaning in his symbols? If he asserts two times two is five, I must ask not what kind of psychosis does this indicate, but can I discover what meaning it has for him to assert this? Only thus will he eventually be helped to give it up.

A psychotherapist colleague of mine remarks that he alternates as in a tennis game between seeing the patient as object—when he thinks of patterns, dynamics, reality testing, and other aspects of general principles to which the patient's behavior refers—and as subject, when he empathizes with the patient's suffering and sees the world through the patient's eyes.

The same is true in our day-to-day living. If I try to act as "pure subject," free and untrammeled by the finite requirements of traffic lights and the engineering principles of how fast my car can negotiate the curve, I of course come to grief—and generally not so nobly or theatrically as Icarus. If on the other hand I set out to deal with myself as "pure object," fully determined and manipulatable, I become driven, dried up, affectless, and unrelated to my experiences. And then my body generally jolts me into remembering that I am not a mechanical object by bringing me down with a case of flu or a heart attack. Curiously enough, both these alternatives—being "purely free" and "purely determined"—amount to the same kind of playing god in the respect that we arrogantly refuse to accept the dilemma which is our fate and our great potentiality as human.

Now to sharpen our definition: we are not simply describing two alternate ways of behaving. Nor is it quite accurate to speak of our being subject and object *simultaneously*. The important point is that our consciousness is a process of oscillation between the two. Indeed, is not this dialectical relationship between experiencing myself as subject and as object just what consciousness consists of? The process of oscillation gives me potentiality—I can choose between them, can throw my weight on one side or the other. However we may alternate in dealing with someone else—say, a patient in therapy—when we are dealing with ourselves, it is the gap between the two ways of responding that is important. My freedom, in any genuine sense, lies not in my capacity to live as "pure subject," but rather in my capacity to experience *both* modes, to live in the dialectical relationship.[1]

Since a number of authors, including myself, have endeavored elsewhere to describe this capacity in greater detail, I shall not go into its infinitely wide implications here. I shall only add that this hiatus between subject and object underlies our experience of time and indicates why time is such an important dimension for human beings. It is the experience of a distance between subject and object, a creative void which must be taken account of and filled. We do this by *time*—we say: "Today" I am here; "tomorrow" I will be there. By the same token, it is in the experiencing of this dialectical relation between subject and object that human language, mathematics, and other forms of symbolization are born and developed. The interrelation between language and our experience of time is thus exceedingly interesting: language becomes possible because of our capacity to "keep" time—we experience a gap which we must do something about. Language also gives us power over time—we say "today," "tomorrow"; we plan our lives for "next" week and year. And we can even take that amazing ultimate step in the consciousness of a subject who is aware that he is also object, anticipate in future time our own death—i.e., "I know that at some future moment I shall cease to be."

This dilemma was unforgettably imprinted on my mind in a conversation a dozen years ago with the physicist Werner Heisenberg. When we were together in an automobile for a several hours' trip at a conference, I seized the opportunity to ask him to explain to me his principle of indeterminacy. A genial person, he complied. In the course of his discussion he emphasized his belief that our classical, inherited view of nature as an object "out there" is an illusion, that the subject is always part of the formula, that the man viewing nature must be figured in, the experimenter into his experiments or the artist into the scene he paints. This subject-object polarity, he indicated, was what he and Niels Bohr call the "principle of complementarity." At this point he dropped an aside, "Of course, you psychologists in your discipline have always known this." I smiled to myself, not wanting to interrupt his discourse; but I had the uneasy feeling that the inseparable relation between subject and object he was describing was exactly what much contemporary psychology had been trying strenuously to avoid.[2]

Our dilemma has been expressed in many ways by biologists, philosophers, theologians and artists. Even though the language of some of these I shall now cite is certainly not psychological, they nevertheless represent serious formulations of phenomena which psychology must take into account and in some way come to terms with. Kurt Goldstein, on the basis of his neurobiological studies, described this phenomenon as man's capacity to transcend the concrete, immediate situation of which he is inescapably a part and to think in abstract terms—i.e., to think in terms of "the possible." Goldstein held, in company with many investigators in the area, that this capacity is what distinguishes man from animals and inanimate nature in the evolutionary scale.

Paul Tillich, from a philosophical viewpoint, described the dilemma as man's "finite freedom": man is finite in the respects that he is subject to death, illness, limitations of intelligence, perception, experience, and other deterministic forces ad infinitum. But at the same time man has freedom *to relate to* these forces; he can be aware of them, give them meaning, and select and throw his weight in favor of this or that force operating on him. Reinhold Niebuhr, from a more theological viewpoint, describes the phenomenon as arising from the fact that human experience combines both "nature" and "spirit," and man functions in both these dimensions simultaneously.

The Swiss biologist Adolph Portmann describes man as characterized by "world openness." That is to say, though man is tied to his natural environment in an infinite number of ways on the one hand, he is able on the other hand to exercise freedom of movement with relation to this environment. There is an evolutionary progression here: trees and plants possess little freedom of movement in relation to their environments; animals, with locomotion and new sense developments, possess greater range of movement. But the worm is still tied to the worm's world and the deer to the world of its forest, whereas in man there emerges a radical new dimension of world openness. "The free play of the limbs," writes Portmann, "which gives to the human nursling so much richer possibilities than the new born monkey or ape have reminds us that our own state at birth is not simply helpless but is characterized by a significant freedom." [3] It is by virtue of the emergence of consciousness that man possesses this radically new dimension of world openness, freedom of movement in relation to the objective environment. And particularly important for our discussion here, man's capacity to be self-aware of the fact that he is both bound and free gives the phenomenon the genuine character of a dilemma, in which some decision must be made, if only to refuse to take responsibility for the freedom involved in this world openness.

The artists, of course, have intimately lived in this human dilemma ever since a caveman first seized reeds and colors and struggled with the recalcitrant conditions of paint and cave walls and forms, trying to make a picture communicate his subjective experience of the bison or reindeer. Eugene O'Neill describes the dilemma as that of biological determinism, which he calls Force or Fate, over against man's capacity to mold the determinism. In 1925 he wrote in a letter:

> I'm always acutely conscious of the Force and of the one eternal tragedy of Man in his glorious, self-destructive struggle to make the Force express him instead of being, as an animal is, an infinitesimal incident in its expression. And my proud conviction is that this is the only subject worth writing about and that it is possible—or can be—to develop a tragic expression in terms of transfigured modern values and symbols in the theatre which may to some degree bring home to members of a modern audience their ennobling identity with the tragic figures on the stage.[4]

IT IS ONE THING, of course, for Eugene O'Neill and the artists to thrive on this dilemma; but it is quite another thing to bring the phenomenon into psychological science. The dilemma we are roughly blocking out has been understandably an embarrassment and in some ways a scandal to psychology. Endeavoring to construct empirical scientific systems, the psychologist finds himself hurled immediately into a caldron of self-contradiction. The more strenuously he tries to be "purely objective" about his data and his work, the more he is caught in subjectivity, deny it though he may. One formulation of the dilemma is given by Morris R. Cohen: "Unlike the physicist, the psychologist . . . investigates processes that belong to the same order —perception, learning, thinking—as those by which he conducts his investigation."[5]

The difficulty psychology falls into by overlooking or trying to avoid this dilemma is illustrated by a letter I received just as I was writing this introductory chapter. The letter, from colleagues in an excellent university department of psychology, informed me that my name was picked in a sampling of members of the American Psychological Association. Would I please participate in their study by checking a scale on the enclosed card? The position on one end of the card was as follows:

> I stood at the window of the nursery and looked at the newborns. How varied they appear when one looks closely! If one could know the dimensions to measure, one could see here the beginnings of individual styles that show themselves persistently through life.

The opposite position was:

> I stood at the window of the nursery and looked at the newborns. I smiled when I caught myself watching one and imagining his 'personality.' How foolish to suppose that dimensions of personal style one could conceivably measure in the nursery would persist through the myriad of encounters awaiting the child, the adolescent, the young adult.

I was asked to check whether I agreed fully with one position or the other, or at what point my opinion fell on a scale between the two.

Now the only trouble with such a scale is that these positions are not at all opposites. A patient of mine who had just become a father related that the obstetrician, coming out of the delivery room, remarked to him, "You've got a long baby there—he'll be a tall fellow." Obviously that father, and any of us looking at babies objectively, will know that physical size, neurological equipment, and other elements that are given at the time and can to some extent be measured will have some influence on the style of the baby throughout life. But just as obviously, and just as soundly, the father, and any of us when identifying with one of the babies subjectively, would be preoccupied with the powerful experiences in his unknown future (atomic war? radiation?) which will radically change his development and can even countermand the originally given physical equipment. How I check my colleagues' scale depends on how I choose my relationship with the new-borns at the time. If I am in my working clothes and lecturing to a class in psychology, I will tend to think in the "predictable" position—and woe to the student who fails to realize that he should check something near that pole if he is trying to get into a graduate school!

What is wrong with the questionnaire is not the details; it is the whole basic presupposition. The two poles are not opposites but two dimensions in which we think and experience all the time. I was being asked to abstract myself from my human experience and to assume a role; and what such a test picks up is not the judgments or experience of the respondents, but the roles they assume.

In this exceedingly difficult and in some ways unresolvable situation, it is not surprising that those of us who have chosen to be psychologists experience a considerable amount of intellectual insecurity and even defensiveness about our science. I am arguing that this insecurity cannot be avoided without doing violence to our material, namely, the human being. The great concern with methodology in psychology seems to be related to this insecurity, as does the hope—which I believe in the long run must surely be illusory for us as it was for the physicists—that if we can only find the right method, we shall be freed from the human dilemma. Thus some therapists, for example, advocate asking not the question that will enable us best to understand our human subject, but the question that will elicit the quantitative answer that best fits our method and system.

Now I am certainly aware, if I may say so without sounding patronizing, that the compelling need for honesty is one of the motives which leads psychologists to seek quantitative measures, the need to find out whether we really do understand the human being better, and to seek formulations which are not dependent on our own subjective criteria. I am also aware that research in our day has to be carefully set up so that the results are teachable and can be built upon by others. The compelling drive to get at the truth is what improves us all as psychologists, and is part and parcel of intellectual integrity. But I do urge that we not let the drive for honesty put blinders on us and cut off our range of vision so that we miss the very thing we set out to understand—namely, the living human being. We must go beyond the naiveté of the faith that if we can only get somehow and ultimately to the "bare empirical facts" we shall at last have arrived safe and sound in the harbor. Professor Feigl does well to remind us that our embarrassments are not so easily overcome. "I will only suggest," he states, "that radical empiricism has a good deal to do with the wish for intellectual security, i.e., with the desire to restrict one's extrapolations to the domain in which they have been thoroughly tested. . . . Hypothesis-phobia has often been a personality trait of positivists." [6]

To show some of the questions and problems that arise from what I am calling the human dilemma, I wish to refer, albeit only briefly here, to the debates between the two psychologists who are widely known as the representatives of the two horns of this dilemma, B. F. Skinner and Carl Rogers.[7] Out of his work in operant conditioning, Professor Skinner proposes that the dilemma—or "bifurcation," as he calls it—can be avoided by the universal application of his behavioristic assumptions and methods. "By arguing that the individual organism simply reacts to its environment, rather than to some inner experience of that environment, the bifurcation of nature into physical and psychic properties can be avoided."[8] In other places he argues for the necessity and inevitability of external control over man, stating that "inner control" is irrelevant, and—though I do not know whether he takes the full implications of this statement into account—"outer control and inner control are the same thing."[9]

Yes, one could avoid the bifurcation precisely by omitting one side of the dilemma, subjective experience, and then—since subjective experience refuses to stay erased—by simply subsuming it under "outer control." Or at least one can do this on paper and in specially controlled laboratory and hospital situations. But if I may ask a naive question, based on what we see demonstrated every moment in psychotherapy, is it not a fact that people *do* react to an inner experience of their environment, *do* see their environment in terms of their past experience, and *do* interpret it in terms of their own symbols, hopes and fears?

When Skinner holds that in education, furthermore, the "child can be molded as the potter does his clay," our rejoinder is not that this is impossible. It does work to some extent and in certain given situations. But does not this point of view leave out significant experience that will return to haunt us—leave out of the equation, for example, critical subjective motivations in learning, such as those Jerome Bruner calls curiosity and Robert White calls desire for competence? Every time I hear the potter-clay metaphor applied to human beings, I brace myself against a clap of thunder and the charge of *nimis simplicandum* hurled across the heavens like a bolt of lightning from Mount Olympus.

This troubling question also arises when we read Skinner's interesting debate (posthumously, at least for one of the parties) with Dostoevsky:

> The study of human behavior [writes Skinner] also answers the cynical complaint that there is a plain "cussedness" in man which will always thwart efforts to improve him. . . . Dostoevsky claimed to see some plan in it. "Out of sheer ingratitude," he complained, or possibly boasted, "man will play you a dirty trick, just to prove that men are still men and not the keys of a piano. . . . And even if you could prove that a man is only a piano key, he would still do something out of sheer perversity— he would create destruction and chaos—just to gain his point. . . . And if all of this could in turn be analyzed and prevented by predicting that it would occur, then man would deliberately go mad to prove his point."

Skinner then proceeds to give his own reaction to the Russian novelist's assertion.

> This is a conceivable neurotic reaction to inept control. A few men may have shown it, and many have enjoyed Dostoevsky's statement because they tend to show it. But that such perversity is a fundamental reaction of the human organism to controlling conditions is sheer nonsense.[10]

Now one must first clear out the question-begging implications of certain words Professor Skinner uses. Let us assume that Dostoevsky is neither "complaining" nor "boasting," but trying to state a point he believes important. We also must not be misled by Professor Skinner's disposing of an opponent by psychopathological diagnosis, an error of which we psychotherapists are generally accused, i.e., labeling Dostoevsky's statement a "neurotic reaction" and holding that those who "enjoy it" (which I am frank to say includes me) also show the "neurotic reaction." Beyond that, Professor Skinner's answer to Dostoevsky is, "sheer nonsense."

But we recall that this is the Dostoevsky who gave us the breathtakingly profound characterizations in *The Brothers Karamazov* and the marvelously subtle picture of psychological development in *Crime and Punishment* and who is by common consent one of the greatest students and portrayers of human experience in all history. Must there not be something radically wrong with a solution to the dilemma that requires, or permits, Dostoevsky to be dismissed as "sheer nonsense"? And we turn from the argument with the conviction that long after our present psychological methods are relegated to dusty archives and replaced again and again by new methods, Dostoevsky's work will go serenely on, revealing to generation after generation its profound wisdom about human experience.

Carl Rogers, on the other side of the platform in the debates, has consistently and firmly argued that it is the inner control which is significant, "client centered" as he is rather than environment centered. Rogers has always believed that if you give the patient the right human relationship—that is, one marked by "congruence," respect, acceptance of all feelings—then the patient will grow quite naturally toward maturity, responsibility and other usually accepted goals of therapy. Rogers has been described as Rousseauesque, and he has readily accepted the classification. In different ways he states over and over again his belief that the human being is "exquisitely rational," and will choose what is rationally best for him if he is given the right opportunity. This all adds up to an emphatic statement of the other side of the dilemma.

But I should like to raise several questions. My queries are based mainly upon my observations as one of the ten judges of the therapy in Rogers' recent four-year research project at the University of Wisconsin in client-centered therapy with schizophrenics.

In listening to tapes of this therapy, I was struck by the fact that whereas the Rogerian therapists were very good at reflecting the loneliness, resignation, abandonment, sadness, and so on, of the patient, they practically never reflected the anger of the patient. Other negative emotions, such as aggression, hostility, and genuine conflict (as distinguished from mere misunderstanding) were also almost absent in what the therapist responded to on the tapes. I found my-self asking, did these patients *never* feel rage? Surely feelings of hostility and expressions of desire to fight can never be wholly ab-sent in a person except in almost complete pathology. And they were not absent, it turned out, in these patients: occasionally in the tapes a patient was enraged at hospital personnel or at the thera-pist himself. But the therapist almost always failed to see this, but interpreted the affect as loneliness or being misunderstood even though the patient would try to make his emotion clear with angry and profane expletives.

Other judges of these tapes also remarked on the therapists' failure to perceive or respond to the aggressive, negative emotions. And in-deed, Rogers and his co-workers are led themselves to ask about this point in their summary of all the judges' clinical reviews:

> Particularly striking was the almost common observation that the client centered process of therapy somehow avoided the ex-pected and usual patient expressions of negative, hostile, or aggressive feelings. The implicit suggestion is clear that the client centered therapist for some reason seemed less open to receiving negative, hostile or aggressive feelings. Is it that the therapists have little respect for, or understanding of their own negative, hostile or aggressive feelings, and are thus unable to adequately perceive those feelings in the patient?

We need, therefore, to put the question, Does not Rogers' empha-sis on rationality, and his belief that the individual will simply choose what is *rational* for him, leave out a large section of the spectrum of human experience, namely, all the *irrational* feelings? Granted that it is not "exquisitely rational" to bite the hand that feeds you, yet that is just what clients and patients do—which is one reason they need therapy. And furthermore, this anger, aggressive-ness, and hostility often express the patient's most precious effort toward autonomy, his way of trying to find some point at which he can stand against the authorities who have always suffocated his life—suffocated it by "kindness" as well as exploitation.

Our point is that the overemphasis upon the subjective, freedom pole of the human dilemma, and the neglect of man as determined object, is also an error. Rogers may partly agree, at least in theory, with this point. In a recent paper, written after the research referred to above, he discusses what he calls the "paradox" of human experience:

> It is my conviction that a part of modern living is to face the paradox that, viewed from one perspective, man is a complex machine. . . . On the other hand, in another dimension of his existence, man is subjectively free; his personal choice and responsibility account for his own life; he is in fact the architect of himself. . . . If in response to this you say, "But these views cannot both be true," my answer is, "This is a deep paradox with which we must learn to live." [11]

True indeed. But it cannot be discerned from this paper whether Rogers is aware that this statement changes his whole previous assumption that man is "exquisitely rational" and will always choose the "right" thing if he has the chance. For if we admit the above paradox, we can no longer talk about simple "growth" as the basic need of the human being, for growth is always within a dialectical relationship in a dilemma that is never fully resolved.[12] What then *is* the "right" thing? It is one thing if you view it from the point of view of freedom and subjectivity: Gauguin runs out on his banking job and family and goes off to Tahiti to paint—and it is easy enough three-quarters of a century later when his paintings are blue-chip financial investments to overlook how irresponsible his "freedom" must have seemed at the time. But how about the "right" thing from the viewpoint of the man who, in quite un-Gauguin fashion, wants to be adjusted to his banker's life, wants to be helped to be a successful social object in his society? I am not implying we must end up simply with cultural and moral relativities—that also is too easy a solution to do justice to the human situation. I am proposing, rather, that we have critically oversimplified our view of ourselves and our fellows, and that we must bring into our picture the dilemma in human experience.

We may foreshadow some of our future discussion by mentioning here that the above considerations cast light on why Kierkegaard and Nietzsche make so much of *commitment*. The very fact of your commiting yourself to one side or the other in a paradox adds a new "force" which was not present before, and which cannot be encompassed in a simple concept of growth. When the person chooses to act, already a new element is added to the motivational pattern; and we cannot know the measure or direction of this force until the person does choose to act.

In this introductory chapter, I have described the human dilemma as the capacity of man to view himself as object and as subject. My point is that both are necessary—necessary for psychological science, for effective therapy, and for meaningful living. I am also proposing that *in the dialectical process between these two poles lies the development, and the deepening and widening, of human consciousness.* The error on both sides—for which I have used Skinner and the pre-paradox Rogers as examples—is the assumption that one can avoid the dilemma by taking one of its poles. It is not simply that man must learn to live with the paradox—the human being has *always* lived in this paradox or dilemma, from the time that he first became aware of the fact that *he* was the one who would die and coined a word for his own death. Illness, limitations of all sorts, and every aspect of our biological state we have indicated are aspects of the deterministic side of the dilemma—man is like the grass of the field, it withereth. The awareness of this, and the acting on this awareness, is the genius of man the subject. But we must also take the implications of this dilemma into our psychological theory. Between the two horns of this dilemma, man has developed symbols, art, language, and the kind of science which is always expanding in its own presuppositions. The courageous living within this dilemma, I believe, is the source of human creativity.[13]

It is considerations of this kind which we shall deal with in the chapters that follow.

NOTES FOR CHAPTER 1

1. It is within this gap that the distinctively human form of anxiety occurs—the anxiety which is the "dizziness of freedom," as Kierkegaard puts it. The neurotic tries to avoid anxiety by abandoning himself to irresponsible freedom or by the opposite way of obsessionally controlling every little action. But neither way works. The healthy person is he who chooses within the gap. When he sets out to paint a picture, for example, he frees himself to let his vision, his phantasies, his irrational urges come into play. When he studies for a final examination, on the other hand, he puts himself into the well-controlled, objective, externally directed mode.

2. A refreshing exception is the research of Robert Rosenthal at Harvard on "experimenter bias" in psychology. Rosenthal enlisted three groups of graduate students to participate in an experiment running rats through a maze. He instructed the first group of students that the rats given them were particularly intelligent, the second group were told nothing about the animals, and the third group that their rat subjects were especially dull. Actually the rats were all "naive," i.e., of the same capability or lack of it. However, the rats of the first group did significantly better on the maze, those of the third group (the supposed dull ones) did worse, again to a distinctly significant degree.

   Rosenthal and colleagues have replicated this experiment in many different forms, including experiments with human subjects. There is no doubt that the experimenter's "bias," or expectation, *does* influence the performance of the subjects, despite the fact that every precaution was taken to make sure the different experimenters gave exactly the same directions to their subjects.

   How is the expectation of the experimenter then communicated to the rats and other subjects? It seems most likely by bodily movement. Rosenthal is now trying to determine by studying movies of such experiments what gets communicated. It would seem also to me that tone of voice, inflection, and infinitely variegated subliminal language with which we communicate without knowing it would be significant.

3. Adolph Portmann, *Biologische Fragmente zu einer Lehre vom Menschen,* Basel, 1951, p. 30. I am indebted to Ernst Schachtel for some helpful discussion of Portmann and for this quotation. Cf. Ernst Schachtel, *Metamorphosis,* Basic Books, New York, 1959, p. 71. Other German biologists, such as J. von Uexküll and V. von Weizsäcker,

have come from different approaches to conclusions similar to Portmann's.

4. Letter to Arthur Hobson Quinn, quoted in Doris V. Falk, *Eugene O'Neill and the Tragic Tension,* Rutgers University Press, New Brunswick, N.J., 1958, pp. 25-26. O'Neill uses the term "self-destructive," but it is clear that he means at the same time that it is the most *constructive* struggle, the struggle by which, and only by which, an individual achieves selfhood and creates significance as well as beauty in his life.

5. Morris R. Cohen, *Reason and Nature,* Free Press, Glencoe, Ill., 1953, p. 81. In a later chapter we come back to the question of the practical consequences this has for psychological science.

6. In an address at the American Psychological Association's annual convention. H. Feigl, "The Philosophical Embarrassments of Psychology," *American Psychologist,* 14:125-126, 1959.

7. We shall come back to the work of Skinner and Rogers in Chapter 14.

8. *Scientific Monthly,* November 1954.

9. *Science,* November 1956.

10. B. F. Skinner, "Freedom and the Control of Man," *American Scholar,* Winter 1955-56, Vol. 25, No. 1.

11. Carl Rogers, "Freedom and Commitment," paper delivered at San Francisco State College, 1963.

12. By the same token, Rogers has always rejected the full implications of Freud's concepts of resistance and repression—concepts which seem to me very important expressions of the human dilemma.

13. "O'Neill believed . . . that for living men the true 'reconciliation' of the opposites was to live them deeply and endure them courageously"—*Op. cit.,* p. 24. It seems that the artists have always intuitively known this. Rainer Maria Rilke writes in his letter to the young poet, "Do not now seek the answers, that cannot be given you because you would not be able to live them. And the point is, to live everything. *Live* the questions now. Perhaps you will then gradually, without noticing it, live along some distant day into the answer"—Rainer Maria Rilke, *Letters to a Young Poet,* translated by M. D. Herter Norton, W. W. Norton & Co., New York, 1934.

Part One

Our Contemporary Situation

In certain historical periods the dilemmas of life become more pronounced, more difficult to live with, and harder to resolve. Our period, the middle of the twentieth century, is one such time. If the reader will accept this thesis tentatively, we shall propose in the next two chapters some ways these dilemmas show themselves.

2

Modern Man's Loss of Significance

> Man is only a reed, the feeblest reed in nature, but he
> is a thinking reed. There is no need for the entire
> universe to arm itself in order to annihilate him: a
> vapor, a drop of water, suffices to kill him. But were
> the universe to crush him, man would yet be more
> noble than that which slays him, because he knows that
> he dies, and the advantage the universe has over him; of
> this the universe knows nothing. Thus all our dignity
> lies in thought. By thought we must raise ourselves, not
> by space and time, which we cannot fill. Let us strive,
> then, to think well—therein is the principle of morality.
> —BLAISE PASCAL, Pensées

In a period of transition, when old values are empty and traditional mores no longer viable, the individual experiences a particular difficulty in finding himself in his world. More people experience
more poignantly the problem of Willie Loman in *The Death of a
Salesman,* "He never knew who he was." The basic dilemma, inhering in human consciousness, is part of all psychological experience
and present in all historical periods. But in times of radical cultural
change, as in sexual mores and religious beliefs, the particular dilemmas which are expressions of the basic human situation become
harder to negotiate.[1]

To begin with, I pose the question, Is not one of the central problems of modern Western man that he experiences himself as without
significance as an individual? Let us focus on that aspect of his
image of himself which is his doubt whether he can act and his
half-aware conviction that even if he did act it would do no good.

25

This is only one side of contemporary man's picture of himself, but it is a psychologically critical aspect—a self-doubt which reflects the tremendous technological power that surges up every moment about him to dwarf overwhelmingly his own puny efforts.

This is a cultural evolution of the problem of "identity" which was brought out with special cogency in the 1950's in the writings of such analysts as Erickson and Wheelis. Persons of all sorts these days, especially younger people, diagnose their trouble when they come to a counselor or therapist as an "identity crisis"—and the fact that the phrase has become trite should not lead us to overlook the fact that it may also be importantly true. "Nowadays the sense of self is deficient. The questions of adolescence—'Who am I?' 'Where am I going?' 'What is the meaning of life?'—receive no final answers. Nor can they be laid aside. The uncertainty persists," wrote Allen Wheelis in 1958.[2] He goes on with respect to the technological progress in our day in culture and in health, "But as our span of years has increased, our span of significant time has diminished."

My thesis is that the problem of identity in the 1950's has now become, more specifically, the crisis of the loss of the sense of significance. It is possible to lack a sense of identity and still preserve the hope of having influence—"I may not know who I am, but at least I can make them notice me." In our present stage of loss of sense of significance, the feeling tends to be, "Even if I did know who I am, I couldn't make any difference as an individual anyway."

I wish to cite as an example of this loss of individual significance, a series of incidents which expressed something important for persons all over the country. I refer to the "revolt" as its enemies labeled it, or "passive resistance" as the students called it, on the Berkeley campus of the University of California. Whatever the complex and subtle factors underlying this protest, it seems agreed on all sides that it was a welling up in students of profound and powerful resistance against the "facelessness of students in the modern factory university." The mood is shown excellently in the fiery rhetoric of Mario Savio, the senior in philosophy who led the massive sit-in which was the occasion for the arrests:

> There is a time when the operation of the machine [of collectivized education] becomes so odious, makes you so sick at heart that you can't take part . . . you've got to put your bodies upon the gears and upon the wheels, upon the levers, upon all the apparatus and you've got to make it stop. . . .

Further evidence that the deep substratum of students' emotions coming then into eruption was the protest against their being treated as anonymous cogs in the wheels of a tremendous system is seen in the reasons many students gave for the value of the protests. After the demonstrations several persons who had participated remarked to me with considerable emotion, "Everybody now speaks to everybody else on the campus." No clearer statement could be made of the fact that what was at stake was the unbearable situation of "nobody knows my name," "I am without significance." It is, indeed, one of the clear values of being a rebel, as Camus and countless others in human history have said and as I shall try to indicate later in this book, that by the act of rebelling I force the impersonal authorities or the too systematic system to look at me, to recognize me, to admit that I *am,* to take account of my *power.* That last word is not underlined for purposes of rhetoric: I mean, literally, that unless I can have some effect, unless my potency can be exercised and can matter, I inevitably will be the passive victim of outside forces and I shall experience myself as without significance.

Since this experience of student insignificance is of importance for what follows in this book, let us note some evidence that the "facelessness of the education factory" is not at all a projection of students' neurotic or subjective phantasy.

> At Berkeley, as on so many other state university campuses, the image of a "factory" is no longer a joke. Berkeley's student population totals nearly 27,500. With a full time faculty of 1,600, some of whom are on leave or engaged in research, the effective student-faculty ratio is approximately 18 to 1, according to university officials.
> The most eminent members of Berkeley's faculty are frequently so absorbed in research that they have little time for students. The younger professors, facing a "publish or perish" battle to stay on at Berkeley, likewise have little time for students. The teaching burden falls heavily on teaching assistants who are

usually inexperienced graduate students working toward their degrees. . . .

One of the many ironies of the Berkeley situation is that much of what has developed was clearly foreseen by President Kerr in his book, "The Uses of the University," published in 1963. Dr. Kerr, an expert in industrial relations with a national reputation as a labor mediator, warns against the "incipient undergraduate revolt," against the "faculty in absentia" and the frustration of students smothering "under a blanket of impersonal rules." In what now reads like the understatement of the Berkeley crisis, Dr. Kerr, who has been university president since 1958, warned, "The students also want to be treated as distinct individuals." [3]

It should be clear also that the contemporary phenomenon of student revolt is not "caused" by some special evil men sitting in the Presidents' offices or on the Boards of Trustees of the universities. That the students themselves see the impersonal source of the evil is shown in many student editorials like the following:

A University of Illinois student columnist, writing in the Daily Illini, called for more student participation in the planning of a new building to be paid for in part by student funds. "It is our job, as concerned students . . . to help save this wonderful organism, the university, from its own efficiency," he wrote, adding, ". . . the loss of a building is nothing compared to the loss of the sense of community here." [3]

What is occurring is an inescapable phenomenon of our times, the inevitable result of the collectivism, mass education, mass communication, mass technology, and the other "mass" processes which form modern people's minds and emotions.

That these are no flash-in-the-pan episodes is shown by the fact that despite the all-university committee's recommendation of the reforms the students demanded, a new apathy has come over the campus, according to Dr. Kerr, from which he warns new protests will spring.[4]

What is the deeper conflict underlying the profound student unrest? Dr. Kerr formulates it as the dilemma arising from the increasing withdrawal of faculty into specialized research at a time when "more students . . . want to gain from their education a personal and social philosophy as well as or even instead of a vocational skill." Dr. Rosemary Park, President of Barnard College, describes the "dangerous times" the university is now in "when student dissatisfaction with education has never been more strident nor faculty disinterest in the institution they serve more apparent." [4] No wonder present graduate students at Berkeley are proclaiming that the only way to restore a meaningful tradition in university life is for the students to conduct "intellectual guerrilla warfare"— a curiously contradictory but significant phrase—against those universities that were set up solely to meet "the operational needs of the corporations and government" rather than "the needs of the moral man." [4] The upshot of all of this is a new and highly important form of the battle for human values against the sophisticated mechanical Moloch of education which threatens to devour what is most precious to each one of us, our imagination and our consciousness itself. It is indeed interesting that in this battle the *moral* demand and cry comes from the students and not the faculty!

Now it is important to recall that these students were brought up, as all of us were in this country from the time of the frontiersman on, to believe that the individual is the one who counts, that his power is decisive in the long run, and that in a democracy it is the individual's say which determines policy. Now they find themselves part of vast factorylike processes which seem to run autonomously and under their own satanically impersonal power. The "mass" processes are a characteristic of the transitional historical period in which we live, and I see no simple detour around the crises which have resulted and the revolts which will still occur. They are symptomatic of the dislocation of human consciousness in our time; they express the struggle of human beings—in this case particularly the students—to resolve the dilemmas so far as possible or to come to terms with them when resolution is impossible.

THE DILEMMAS WE CONFRONT, thus, are sharpened by the contemporary cultural and historical upheavals of Western civilization, upheavals which make it inevitable that the self-image of the individual will be greatly shaken. Robert and Helen Lynd wrote about the confusion of role of the individual in *Middletown* three decades ago; the citizen is "caught in a chaos of conflicting patterns, no one of them wholly condemned, but no one of them clearly approved and free from confusion; or where the group sanctions are clear in demanding a certain role of a man or woman, the individual encounters cultural requirements with no immediate means of meeting them." The Lynds related this to socioeconomic upheaval in Middletown in the 1930's, but I believe a greater and more fundamental conflict of roles—an experience of *absence* of any viable roles—is occurring in our present world three decades later. Lacking positive myths to guide him, many a sensitive contemporary man finds only the model of the machine beckoning him from every side to make himself over into its image. The protests we hear are the clashing sounds of the struggle—agonizing, often despairing, but never relinquished—against this latter-day Circe.

The most striking symbol for the individual's sense of insignificance is, of course, the ever-present specter of thermonuclear war. So far as I can observe, people in New York City and over the East —and there is no reason to assume the mood is any different in other parts of the country if we make allowance for cultural lags and pockets of encapsulation—have the belief that they are impotent before this possibility of nuclear war; and the impotence leads to confusion, apathy, and the gnawing conviction, no matter how covered up by diversions or frantic togetherness, "I do not matter." This in turn leads to several vicious circles which we shall now examine. I choose the following example because it so well illustrates the psychological dynamics in this dilemma.

In the fall of 1961 there developed in the East in the face of the threat of thermonuclear war, a curious panic centering around fallout shelters. I say "curious" not because the anxiety itself was unexpected—it followed the panic over the only too real threat of the Berlin crisis—but because of certain psychological symptoms which emerged. During those weeks I participated in several public discussions and debates over radio and television, and I received the weird impression that for many people the fallout shelters represented a crawling back into caves in the earth as an acting out of the conviction that in our helplessness we could only revert to a new womb, our only concern an infantile preoccupation with saving our own skins. Understandably overweighed with their impotence in the crisis, people tended to act as though they could do no more than hope and pray for the luck to avert the holocaust while they themselves, ostrichlike, could only hide underground. Unfortunately the stand of the government in recommending that those who could afford it—which meant the suburban rich—build their private shelters added to the impotence.[5]

I recall that one of my opponents in a radio debate at the time of that panic, an eminent political economist with considerable experience in government, said in answer to a question from one of the several hundred people in the hall, "You cannot have any influence whatever on the question of whether or not there will be war. This is decided entirely by the councils of the few high political leaders who gather in Berlin." This, of course, was exactly what people tended to believe anyway.[6] If they had been a little more convinced of the insignificance of their own acts, they wouldn't have bothered to come out to public discussions like this or even to flick the radio on.

The point I wish to make is that when people feel their insignificance as individual persons, they also suffer an undermining of their sense of human responsibility. Why load yourself with responsibility if what you do doesn't matter anyway, and you must be on edge every moment ready to flee? What vivid symbols of our impotence were these ghastly wounds in the ground! And what a testimony to the disintegration of social values was our being adjured to dig the caves at night to keep our neighbors from knowing where they were, so that in the time of peril one man, with two or three of his family gathered around him, could crawl into the cave and there gain some sort of isolated protection! (The protection was mostly illusory anyway, so we were later informed by the physicists who knew about the inevitable fire storms.) Or a cement ready-made shelter could be purchased, as it was pictured in *Life* and on television, with ventilation tubes from the world above, all the food stored in the walls, coke and a record-player furnished for the teenager and light reading to divert the adults while the bombs fell above on the earth —all for the bargain price of $20,000.

But the most staggering thing of all was that this crawling back into the earth was a protection purchased at the price of the destruction of human love and trust. We all too vividly recall the comforting reassurances from some clergymen and other respectable guardians of the nation's morals that it was ethical to shoot down your neighbor and his children if these unfortunates tried to push into your shelter in their moment of danger and panic.

Thus the impotence in the face of thermonuclear war *moved into anxiety, the anxiety into regression and apathy, these in turn into hostility, and the hostility into an alienation of man from man.* This is the vicious circle that is acted out when our sense of significance is undermined. The only way we can then move is backwards in a psychological regression to an infantile state, a self-chosen encapsulation in our latter-day combination womb-tomb, in which no umbilical cord is necessary since food is stored within the tomb as in the burial caves which Neolithic man built for his journey to the land of the dead.

But the human being never gives up his potency lightly or simply. Anxiety is generated within him in direct proportion to his conviction of his own impotence. What is important here is to emphasize the well-known vicious circle of panic which we have already touched upon—anxiety to apathy to increased hatred to greater isolation of the person from his fellowmen—an isolation which, finally, increases the individual's sense of insignificance and helplessness. Suspicion and enmity toward the neighbor in such times become acceptable and "moral" in ways that would horrify us (and are therefore repressed) in conventional periods. And the hatred and readiness to destroy our own neighbors become in a strange, reverse way—"strange" conventionally but not clinically—an outlet for our own anxiety and impotence. What happens in such moments of anxiety is only the extreme expression of the breakdown of man's sense of significance as an individual and consequently his loss of capacity for individual decision and responsibility.

The war in Vietnam—the "most unwanted war in history," as it has been called—did nothing to dispel the moods of earlier crises or lighten the sense of a profound and troubling impotence. The feeling of impotence was not at all limited to those who were opposed to the conflict but seemed to affect just as insidiously those who believed in and prosecuted the war.

I want to examine this crisis as an illustration of the fact that all of us, whether for or against the war, are caught in a historical situation of upheaval in which there is no clear right and wrong, in which psychological confusion is therefore inescapable, and—a fact which is most frightening of all—no one person or group of persons is in a position to exercise the significant power. Power takes on an anonymous, automatic, and impersonal character.

My purpose here is not political, but to describe as clearly as I can a situation which bears on psychological insignificance, so that we can return to an analysis of that problem. In hearings of the Senate Foreign Relations Committee the same questions were directed over and over to Secretary of State Rusk, Secretary of Defense McNamara, and other persons in the Government, Why were we in Vietnam? What were our real goals? What were our powers there, and what could we realistically expect to accomplish? After reams of testimony (our data is at least plentiful and ready at hand thanks to the mass communication of television and press) Senator Fulbright and other senators, who could by no means be considered stupid or biased about the war, still reported that these questions remain unanswered. "Mr. Fulbright said he had the greatest difficulty," so the *New York Times* reported,[7] "in understanding what the Administration's real objectives were and 'whether what we seek is achievable.' " As Senator Fulbright continually pointed out, and as the representatives of the government did not deny, it was an "open-ended" war; more and more power was poured, always with possibility of the ultimate power of the nuclear bomb in the offing, into a situation in which *by definition we did not and could not have control over the critical decisions.* Newsmen tried in vain to get McNamara to state the long-range plans for the commitment of troops, but he assiduously refused to state more than the pragmatic immediate fact that the Defense Department was "filling the requests of General Westmoreland," and the President, when pushed with similar questions, replied, "I have no unfulfilled requests on my desk."

Now the irony of this situation, not to be obscured by moralistic imputations against this or that Secretary, was that that was all they *could* say. For by the very structure of the situation they did not have control over long-range plans: China and other powers could change these at any moment. The citizen of Minneapolis or Denver who experienced his own lack of significance in this situation might assume, out of an anachronistic psychology of several decades ago, that at least others in Washington were making the significant decisions. But when we looked to Washington we found that *no one* in any final sense had the significant power; everyone, including the President, could plan only within a limited time range and within uncertain variables, for the critical data were simply not available; and the *pragmatic* answer, given by the immediate situation, was about all that could be arrived at.

The dilemma was starkly and tragically real. This dilemma was an inescapable result of the nature of our transitional historical period, when impersonal power has taken on such vast implications and meanings, and human consciousness, responsibility and intentions have not kept up, and probably could not have kept up. I am not making a statement of historical doom, nor do I at all imply that nothing could be done to improve the situation in the Vietnamese war; apathy and passivity are the last things in the world I am proposing.[8] My point is that if our historical situation, and the psychological implications this has for those of us living at this moment, is recognized, we shall be helped to shift our approaches from self-defeating policies to others which at least have some chance of ultimately constructive results. I believe that we have played ostrich with the issue of power, resorting on the one hand to an anachronistic nineteenth-century military psychology, and on the other to self-righteous pacifism. Both were oversimplifications—and to oversimplify in the age of the nuclear bomb is highly dangerous. A widened and deepened consciousness, and a sense of responsibility infused with an imagination which could conceive of new ways of relating to the orient, seem to me necessary for a constructive solution to our problems. But this possibility rests on our confronting the deeper dilemma between the impersonal power of technology on one hand and human values on the other.

In this vacuum of power—that is, the application of greater and greater power (in this case military) to a situation in which one did not have the ultimate significant choice—the real danger was that we would retreat to the only answer available, namely the *pragmatic* answer, the answer that can be given by logistics, the answer that can be arrived at by our computers, the impersonal answer, the answer furnished by the very technology whose unlimited and magnificent spawning had been central in bringing us into the situation in which our force for destruction so vastly exceeded our capacity for significant decision. As I shall indicate below, it is as absurd to "blame" technology—and as scientifically illiterate—as it is absurd morally to blame some "evil" government leaders in other countries —a kind of self-righteousness which leads one into the illusion, so common in psychotherapy, that if only some other persons would change, we would be spared our great problems.

My purpose in this book, to repeat, is not political, but to make as clear as I can how certain important psychological problems arise. A situation of impotence and lack of significance such as has been presented above leads understandably to *confusion* and then to *apathy*. These in turn lead into the vicious circle in psychological dynamics which we have mentioned, and which we shall now explore more deeply.[9]

WHEN THE INDIVIDUAL loses his significance, there occurs a sense of apathy, which is an expression of his state of diminished consciousness. Is not the real danger this surrender of consciousness—the danger that our society will move in the direction of the man who expects the drugs to make him comfortable and the machine not only to satisfy all his needs but in the form of psychoanalytic mechanisms, to make him happy and able to love as well? When

Karl Jaspers talks about the danger of modern man losing his self-consciousness, he is not speaking in hyperbole: we need to take him quite seriously. For this loss is no longer simply a theoretical possibility dreamt up by psychoanalysts or the "morbid existentialist" philosophers.

This diminution of consciousness, I believe, is central to the deepest form of the loss of the sense of significance. What is implied is that this may be the last age of the historical man, that is, the last age in which man *knows* he has a history. Not the last age in which there is a factual history—that is not the point—but the last age in which I can self-consciously stand as a human being who knows that he stands at this point in history, and taking responsibility for this fact, can use the wisdom of the past to illuminate the life and world around me. Such action requires a self-consciousness that can affirm and assert itself, and that in turn requires that I believe in my own significance. It *does* matter then whether I act, and I act in faith that my actions can have some influence.

We have said that the devil of this drama is not technology, and it is absurd to think that if we could throw out technology, we should escape our human dilemmas. On the obvious level, technology is a set of tools, and the important question is, For what purpose are these tools used? On a less obvious level, it is true that technology does shape our image of ourselves in conditioning the kind of information we listen for. But the critical threat with respect to technology does not lie in those two: it is that we succumb to the temptation to use technology as a way of avoiding confronting our own anxiety, our alienation, and our loneliness. When a man is anxious about thermonuclear war, he can hope that with a few more missiles we shall be safe. When anxious about loneliness he can go to a psychoanalyst or learn some new operant conditioning technique, or take some drug, so that, at so much an hour or a dose, he can be changed into the man who will love and be happy. But technology used as a way to evade anxiety makes man even more anxious, more isolated, alienated in the long run, for it progressively robs him of consciousness and his own experiencing of himself as a centered person with significance.

The ultimately self-destructive use of technology consists of employing it to fill the vacuum of our own diminished consciousness. And conversely, the ultimate challenge facing modern man is whether he can widen and deepen his own consciousness to fill the vacuum created by the fantastic increase of his technological power. It seems to me that, and not the outcome of a particular war, is the issue on which our survival hinges.

There is, however, a particular dilemma we need to mention which is made more difficult by modern technology. This is the phenomenon of the "organization man." Increasingly in our time— this is an inevitable result of collectivization—it is the organization man who succeeds. And he is characterized by the fact that *he has significance only if he gives up his significance.* A curious paradox is present in some patients we get in New York City: one gains his status on Madison Avenue at the price of giving up his originality. One becomes the man who works well in an organization, the harmonistic "team man," the worker who maintains a protective coloring so that he won't be singled out and shot at. To this extent you are said to be significant, but it is a significance that is bought precisely at the price of giving up your significance.

The loss of the experience of one's own significance leads to the kind of anxiety that Paul Tillich called the anxiety of meaninglessness, or what Kierkegaard terms anxiety as the fear of nothingness. We used to talk about these things as psychological theories, and a couple of decades ago when I was undergoing my psychoanalytic training, we discussed them as psychological phenomena shown by "neurotic" people. Now such anxiety is endemic throughout our whole society. These are some of the considerations which impel me to suggest that there is "no hiding place" with respect to the psychological dilemmas of our time. We may as well, then, confront them directly. This we shall now essay to do.

NOTES FOR CHAPTER 2

1. It is easy, of course, to make prophetic generalities about one's age, the purpose often of which is to obfuscate and evade the concrete realities of our immediate daily experience. But we should not allow

our weariness with such generalities to lead us to dull our awareness of what *is* going on around us, to cover up our consciousness
of the meaning and implications of our historical time, or to hide
behind the comfortable and secure stockade of *ex post facto* statistics.
I shall try to make my own beliefs and assumptions as clear as possible as we go along, in the confidence that the reader can best disagree and arrive at his own beliefs in this dialogue if he has no
confusion about mine.

2. Allen Wheelis, *The Quest for Identity,* Norton, New York, 1958,
   pp. 18 and 23.

3. From an editorial, "Berkeley's Lesson," in the *New England Association Review,* the official publication of the New England Association of Colleges and Secondary Schools, Winter 1965, pp. 14-15.

4. Report of consultation on "The University in America," sponsored
   by the Center for the Study of Democratic Institutions, *New York
   Times,* May 10, 1966.

5. President Kennedy became aware that this advocacy of private
   shelters was a mistake, and the recommendation was rescinded in
   two months. I do not have the impression very many private shelters
   were actually built, partly no doubt because people got caught in the
   same psychological vicious circle we are about to explore.

6. My own stand and that of many other people in the audience was,
   of course, radically against my opponent. Let me here only say that
   the reader will see that the point my opponent was raising is one
   of those questions that depends, in its ultimate truth or falsehood,
   exactly on whether or not we *do act.* If we had accepted my opponent's statement, we would remain passive; and his statement
   would become true by virtue of our accepting it. If, on the other
   hand, we refused to accept it, but did what little we could to influence Congress, the President, and other leaders, then even a group
   as small as this several hundred—and certainly the thousands listening on the radio—could have some significance, infinitesimally small
   as it may be to begin with. This is the point where political freedom
   begins, as I shall indicate later.

7. *New York Times,* March 4, 1966.

8. I have myself been continually concerned with action on these issues,
   because I believe that social apathy is our central danger. My own
   personal opinion was that, regardless of how and why we got into
   Vietnam, we could not simply pull out. I believe power confers
   responsibility, and it would have been irresponsible for a nation of
   our power to play ostrich in the East, or to fail to realize that we
   have tremendous influence in every section of the world whether

we choose to exercise it in an enlightened way or not. I believe that our perpetual nonrecognition of Communist China was an example of playing ostrich. The widened and deepened consciousness which will be necessary for solutions to our problems will have to include, in my judgment, a fresh way of perceiving other nations like China, as well as other races.

9. Though later in this book we shall be discussing the possible answers to these psychological problems, it may be clarifying here briefly to indicate that bringing the political problem into awareness, identifying it, and then frankly confronting it, is already the first step in developing the deepened consciousness that can meet the problem. A sense of responsibility infused with imagination seems to me the first essential. Second, a forming of policy based on *human* goals rather than those given by pragmatic, technological power. Third, a rigorous refusal to let the difficulty of forming long-term goals, as well as the ease of letting our computers form our short-term goals, keep us from devoting thought and energy to the project of long-term aims. We need "some sense of proportion in relating means to ends," write the editors of the journal *Christianity and Crisis*. "What is lacking so far is the willingness to look at realities and the moral imagination to seek better methods than the present contradictory mixture of peaceful rhetoric and stubborn policy"—March 5, 1966.

3

Personal Identity in an Anonymous World

> *When I see a man in a state of anxiety . . . I cannot say that he is no performer on the lyre, but I can say something else of him. . . . And first of all I call him a stranger and say, This man does not know where in the world he is.*
>
> —EPICTETUS (*60-120* A.D.), *"Concerning Anxiety"*

We have noted some problems which arise from the loss of individual significance in the face of the vast and powerful collectivist tendencies in the contemporary scene. This loss forces us all to confront the struggle to find and preserve personal identity in this anonymous world, but the situation imposes an especially painful burden upon students. The "pain" of which I speak—and indeed the common denominator as we all experience it in such dilemmas —is *anxiety*. It is, specifically, anxiety experienced at the threat of the diminution or loss of personal identity. In this chapter I propose to examine this issue, in its relation to the anonymous world of education, but that is but one expression of the broader problem of personal identity in our Western civilization.

I am a clinician, and I always like to begin where the shoe pinches, where the issue hurts. This I think we can do most fruitfully by analyzing the nature and causes of anxiety and then turning to the question of education and personal identity.

Let us first ask, What is anxiety? If someone in the room shouts "Fire!" I suddenly look up, my heartbeat accelerates, my blood

40

pressure rises so that my muscles can work more efficiently, and my senses are sharpened so that I can better perceive the blaze and choose a good way to get out. This is normal anxiety.

But if, as I move toward the door, I see that it is blocked and discover there is no other way out—a situation of "no exit"—my emotional state immediately becomes something quite different. My muscles become paralyzed, my senses are suddenly blurred, and my perception obscured. I cannot orient myself; I feel as though I am in a bad dream; I experience panic. This is neurotic anxiety.

The first is constructive and helps us to meet threatening situations effectively. The second, neurotic anxiety, is destructive. *It consists of the shrinking of consciousness, the blocking off of awareness; and when it is prolonged it leads to a feeling of depersonalization and apathy.* Anxiety is losing the sense of one's self in relation to the objective world. The fact that the distinction between subjectivity and objectivity at that moment is blurred is one aspect of our experience of being immobilized, paralyzed, while in anxiety. Anxiety is losing one's world, and since "self" and "world" are always correlates, it means losing one's self at the same moment.

This unconstructive anxiety is the state to a greater or lesser degree, of those who have lost, or never achieved, the experience of their own identity in the world. We have seen that this is in part due to the vast upheavals in our age economically, politically, morally, and scientifically. There could be no more vivid a situation of "no exit" for many young people than that which they experienced with regard to the war in Vietnam. They faced the prospect of being drafted in a war nobody wanted, to fight for goals nobody knew, in a terrain in which nobody believed a war could be really won, yet it was a war from which we could not withdraw. The confusion of goals in our international relations was itself productive of the uncertainty which makes for the paralysis of anxiety.

But the problem has deeper sources than these sociological and political crises. *Anxiety occurs because of a threat to the values a person identifies with his existence as a self.* In my example above, "fire" is a threat to the value of physical life. But most anxiety comes from a threat to social, emotional, and moral values the person identifies with himself. And here we find that a main source of anxiety, particularly in the younger generation, is that they do not have viable values available in the culture on the basis of which they can relate to their world. The anxiety which is inescapable in an age in which values are so radically in transition is a central cause of apathy; and as I indicated above, such prolonged anxiety tends to develop into lack of feeling and the experience of depersonalization.

One area in which anxiety shows itself is in sexuality and the choosing of a mate. Sex in our day is often used in the service of security: it is the readiest way to overcome your own apathy and isolation. The titillation of the sexual partner is not only an outlet for nervous tension, but demonstrates one's own significance; if a man is able to arouse such feelings in the other, he proves he is alive himself. The "going steady" ("premature monogamy" it has been called) and the tendency toward early marriage of many students are similarly often used in the service of overcoming anxiety—"togetherness" gives at least a temporary security and sense of meaning. But togetherness easily gets empty and boring, particularly when it begins so early the young people have not given themselves the chance to develop their capacities to be interesting as persons. Sex is always something we can do when we run out of conversation. Thus going steady tends toward the meaninglessness of promiscuity, which is the substitution of *bodily intimacy* for *personal relationship*. The "body" is asked to fill the hiatus left when the "person" abdicates. And early marriage, which is the second result of using sex for security, tends toward the equally frustrating emptiness of premature commitment with the haunting possibility of a boring marital future. Both are ways of "shrinking consciousness" at the time, speaking from the viewpoint of psychophysical development, when the young person should be exploring and developing his capacity to know different members of the opposite sex, that he may eventually choose one with whom he has some possibility of a lasting and meaningful partnership.

This use of sex in the service of security tends understandably to make sex increasingly *impersonal*. Indeed, the impersonal element—

one must prove he can perform sexually without getting involved, without commitment—is the element investigators and writers on the problem are most concerned about. The impersonality has the effect of placing a premium on *sensation* without *sensitivity, intercourse* without *intimacy,* and in a strange perverse way makes the denial of feeling a preferred goal. It is exactly this loss of the feeling of being one's self in relation to one's interpersonal world that we are indicating constitutes destructive anxiety.

When I was lecturing at a California college on sex and love, the students informed me that they had had a "computer dance" the night before. My eyes were quizzical with visions of computers dancing with students. But they went on to assure me that it was different from my phantasy: the students had filled out a questionnaire, and the computer had then matched each student with three of the opposite sex. At the party they all went around consulting their IBM cards—no doubt as students in my unenlightened day went around with our dance programs. They told me the dance was an outstanding success because everyone was relieved of his shyness.

While I was on the campus a night club in California also instituted the computer plan. One evening the machine turned out the card of a brunette who was not quite divinely proportioned. As she stood up in front, the machine produced the card of the matching man. But he, apparently thinking the computer's ego-ideal was not high enough for him, did not come up. And the poor girl was left standing, if not at the altar at least in the center of the dance floor. We thought, then, that the night club should be called the house of ill-compute.

The questions I raised with the students were, Is it so good to be "matched" with three persons like you? Is not your college age the time to meet and know many different types of persons of the opposite sex, so that tastes and interests and sensibilities you did not know you had can be born and drawn out? Granted that shyness can be pretty painful (surely neurotic shyness should be gotten over) and that everyone no doubt feels himself too shy, yet is it so good that normal shyness should be entirely erased? *Is not shyness the growing edge of new relationships?* And does shyness not have its normal constructive function, to be sure possibly painful on one side, but zestful and exhilarating on the other, of opening up new areas of experience? Indeed, is not shyness in its normal degree the most *personal* of all emotions? I for one would be very dubious about the pleasure of spending many evenings in circles where no one was ever shy. And I also asked the students, should one not be particularly dubious about letting the computer, thick-aluminum skinned as it is, perform all of your chance-taking and commitment for you?

TURNING NOW to the more specific "causes" of anxiety in education, the most obvious one is the great pressure to get high grades in order to get admitted to college, and the pressure continuing in college to get high grades for admission to graduate school. Parents nag and cajole the students to get those necessary A's, and these days even extracurricular interests in junior high are selected with an eye to how they will look on application blanks. Consequently freshman year often represents a letdown and disappointment to the student: is this what he has devoted so much of his life to for twelve whole years? And is it surprising that students once admitted to graduate school often exhibit a frank cynicism about education and the goals of life? In a letter, Dean Arthur Jensen of Dartmouth put it eloquently: "Each year I can see the pressures of the requirements to get into graduate school beginning to increase. The bright lad who is content with B's in formal courses so he can wallow in the library, walk and watch the stars at night and 'invite his soul'—the lad who has Tillich's 'courage to be'— seems more and more to be the one whose values diverge so much from those of his fellows that he becomes the odd-ball."

The point I am making is not simply that such pressure causes anxiety—everyone and at all stages in life has to face pressure. I am pointing out rather that *the students' values are inevitably shifted to external signs.* He is validated by scores; he experiences himself of worth only in terms of a series of marks on a technical scale. This shift of validation to the outside shrinks his consciousness and undermines his experience of himself. And again it is not simply that the criteria are external (we all must live, at whatever stage, by many external criteria) but rather the criteria are not *chosen by the person himself* but brought to bear upon him by others, in this case parents and school authorities.

One way for the student to meet this anxiety is, of course, to adopt the external values himself, with a healthy admixture of cynicism, and to say, "OK, I'll play the game the way they set it up." He adapts to the educational system with one hand and hopefully preserves his own soul and humanity with the other. Such an attitude has its usefulness, but it is purchased at the price of a cynicism which must be overcome by the development of later values of one's own if it is not to end in apathy.

The admission procedures of colleges and graduate schools of course play a critical, and I fear sometimes definitely destructive, role here. If the IBM machine is the chief member of the admissions committee, the college cannot avoid tending to select those students who best fit the machine; and this inescapably becomes part of the pressure in education to make the student over into the image of the machine.

This brings us to the most serious cause of students' anxiety, namely, certain tendencies within the educational process itself. Learning tends to get increasingly lost behind externalized acquisition of data. Our campuses suffer under the illusion that wisdom consists of the sheer accumulation of facts; the student piles Ossa on Pelion in the frantic endeavor to gain new facts. But what with the "knowledge explosion" these days—what with microfilms, abstracts, endless cross-references, new research, all increasing geometrically every day—the student can never catch up no matter how fast he runs. Indeed, he generally finds himself getting farther and farther behind each day. So the Ph.D. candidate has to work in frantic haste to get his research in, for he never knows which bright morning he will pick up the *New York Times* at his door to find that a new discovery made by Dr. X. here or there on the globe makes his whole approach invalid and washes out all his work.

Dwight Macdonald has put the problem sharply:

Our mass culture—and a good deal of our high, or serious, culture as well—is dominated by an emphasis on data and a corresponding lack of interest in theory, by a frank admiration of the factual and an uneasy contempt for imagination, sensibility and speculation. We are obsessed with technique, hag-ridden by Facts, in love with information. Our popular novelists must tell us all about the historical and professional backgrounds of their puppets; our press lords make millions by giving us this day our daily Facts; our scholars—or, more accurately, our research administrators—erect pyramids of data to cover the corpse of a stillborn idea. . . .[1]

The point I am making is that the externalizing of education in this emphasis upon piling fact upon fact in itself *undermines the experience of identity of the student, and is a prime cause of anxiety.* Where in this is the adventure of thinking, the joy of the stretching of the mind? Indeed, the student's urge to *explore* is lost under the compulsion to *acquire.* The very emphasis upon acquisition itself puts a premium on the student's *not* seeing how he is related to the facts. Such a concern not only takes too much time, but it puts the fact in a new context, makes it partly personal; and who is to say (the grader generally tries to!) that this does not bias the pure fact? Better then to keep your facts and your feelings separate, otherwise you will meditate too much, you will stop to muse, and your "facts" will be tainted with subjectivity.

Students who are grasped by the desire to learn, to follow their original promptings, then experience anxiety at their self-betrayal. The student not only finds himself on an assembly line and faces, as I indicated above, the staggering quantities of data that are bound sooner or later to defeat him; even more important, he tends to lose contact with the inner meaning and significance of what he is studying. The relation of the data to himself as a person, to his consciousness of life, is lost.

Certainly the originality and ingenuity of the student tend to be denied because they are not pragmatically useful; and imagination tends to be bypassed. But it is by my imagination that I can see, relate to, and create my world. And it is by my originality, my experience of myself as this unique pattern of sensibilities who at this instant is experiencing a particular relationship to other people and the world about me, by which I know myself as an identity. Certainly we all have much in common; most of us like the taste of steak and at other moments experience an aesthetic and spiritual thrill in a couplet from Yeats or in gazing at the drawing on a Greek vase. These we share. But it is important that it is *I* experiencing this taste or this joy in the poetry or Greek drawing. And if this "I" experience is lost—lost under the pressure of my trying to remember what my professor said about the poem— soon I shall progressively lose my aesthetic and spiritual sensitivity as well. Education thus plays into the hands of the student's neurotic anxiety and increases it.

An experience of mine which occurred while I was teaching recently at a university may illustrate this point. When I played a recording of a psychotherapeutic interview to my large undergraduate course, the students were able quite readily to hear, and say, that the patient at this point was angry, at that point sad, and so on. But when I played the same interview to my small graduate seminar, composed of students with professional training, they were surprisingly less able to hear and discern the patient's feelings. The naive sophomores and juniors could hear the communication from the patient and perceive what was going on; the sophisticated graduate students, who knew all the dynamics and mechanics of human reactions, gave back to me what they had read in books, formulations of this and that dynamic: their knowledge about human behavior as external discrete facts got in the way of hearing and seeing the person on the tape. This actually made their reactions, empirically speaking, *less* accurate. There was, of course, the competitive factor which made them anxious; undergraduates in a class of a hundred and fifty are not afraid they will be singled out and given a bad grade, but some of the graduate students needed my recommendation to get on to the next graduate program. But our main point holds; in the perpetual piling of fact on fact, the student loses his immediate relation to his subject matter; the formula and testing machine intervene between the student and the human beings he purportedly seeks to understand. There is then greater and greater distance between our senses and our data.

I believe there is something fundamentally wrong in this approach to education. Dr. René J. Dubos of the Rockefeller Institute said that he had reviewed all the important scientific discoveries of the last couple of centuries—such as those of Darwin, Freud, Einstein—and not one of them was made by piling fact on fact. The discoveries are made rather by the scientist's perception of the *significance of relationships, the meaningful pattern among facts.*

Apples have dropped on people's heads since man first stood upright on two legs and walked under apple trees. But Isaac Newton was the one to perceive the significance of this event. And it took only one thump of an apple on Isaac's head. Our contemporary student in his graduate work is hit on the head so many scores of times by academic apples and gets so groggy that his sensitivity and perception are numbed and he has less and less chance of perceiving the significance of what is going on. So all he can do is resign himself to counting how many apples drop and making a nice formula as to the ratio of times they hit his head. From what students say, there lies here, in heads bruised by apples, a dreary commentary on much modern graduate education.

These inevitably depersonalizing processes unfortunately fit much of what we have been teaching for many years. We have been telling students that they are only a reflection of social needs and forces, and it is not surprising that they come to believe it. We have been telling them that they are merely bundles of conditioned reflexes, that freedom and choice are illusions, and they now come to believe it. We should not be surprised, then, that they experience themselves as depersonalized and immobilized, and thereby experience anxiety. I do not, let me hasten to say, imply that any particular psychological or sociological theories are responsible for our historical predicament. Theories and forms of education are *reflections* of our cultural situation as well as causes; and we all, whatever our points of view, share in the responsibility for the problems I am discussing. I am emphasizing, rather, that since a great deal of student anxiety is connected with trends in our culture which have permeated education itself, we do not need to look far afield to understand students' anxiety.

WHEN I WAS invited to lecture on this problem before the presidents and personnel officers of the New England Colleges and Secondary Schools, I was discourteous enough to point out to them that the very way they phrased the topic they gave me reflects the depersonalizing tendencies in our culture. That proposed topic was: "What can the schools and colleges do to reduce anxiety and increase productivity in the learning years?" Take, for example, that phrase "to *reduce* anxiety." In my example of the "fire" at the beginning of this chapter, it would obviously be very unconstructive to *reduce* anxiety, to give the person a tranquilizer under the influence of which he may burn painlessly. The blotting out of consciousness which we have seen occur in neurotic anxiety has exactly the effect of perpetuating anxiety by evading its cause; and I think the tranquilizing mood in our whole culture has a similar cause and effect.

So far as helping students goes, our goal should be to shift anxiety from a neurotic to a constructive form, i.e., to help the student identify what he genuinely fears—and what he should fear—and thereby help him take steps to overcome the threat. And this holds for each of us in his own relation to his own anxiety. It would be irrational for the student, or any of us, *not* to be anxious in the kind of world we live in. "Anxiety is our best teacher," wrote Kierkegaard. And he went on: "I would say that learning to know anxiety is an adventure which every man has to affront if he would not go to perdition either by not having known anxiety or by sinking under it. He therefore who has learned rightly to be anxious has learned the most important thing."

Note also the phrase in the above topic, "increase productivity." I have been trying to say that the overemphasis on productivity in education is exactly a cause of anxiety. *It is the machine which produces; man creates.* For my part I would rather see a cultivation on our campuses of the courage for and possibility of solitude, a rediscovering of meditation, a development of attitudes that will cherish quietness and the opportunity for the student to ponder and think, rather than the emphasis on never-ending productivity. Is there not plenty of evidence that you and I and our students cannot possibly keep up with the machine in producing anyway, particularly with the imminent emergence of cybernetics? Perhaps the machine itself will prove to us that we have no choice but to be human! Then we shall realize—and I trust help our students to realize—that man does something of much greater importance: he can perceive *significance,* can find *meanings.* And with his imagination, he can do what the machine can never do, namely, make the plans and choose the goals.

Thus it seems to me that the main thing necessary to help students and any of us to confront their anxiety constructively is to reconsider the process and ends of education. I am arguing that the overemphasis on the Baconian doctrine of knowledge as power, and the accompanying concern with gaining power *over* nature as well as *over* ourselves in the sense of treating ourselves as objects to be manipulated rather than human beings whose aim is to expand in meaningful living, have resulted in the validation of the self by external criteria—which in effect means the *invalidation* of the self. This tends to shrink the individual's consciousness, to block off his awareness, and thus play into the unconstructive anxiety we saw above. I propose that the aim of education is exactly the opposite, namely, *the widening and deepening of consciousness.* To the extent that education can help the student develop *sensitivity, depth of perception,* and above all the capacity to perceive *significant forms* in what he is studying, it will be developing at the same time the student's capacity to deal with anxiety constructively.

We have seen above that unconstructive anxiety takes over by virtue of shrinking the consciousness of the individual. Hence the widening of consciousness is itself the fundamental way to meet anxiety.

A final point I wish to make has to do with the importance of values. I said at the outset of this chapter that anxiety is the reaction to the threat to values one identifies with his existence as a self. I now add a corollary: *a person can meet anxiety to the extent that his values are stronger than the threat.* This now draws together several implications made throughout this chapter, that basic to the prevalence of destructive anxiety in our day, on campuses as well as in the rest of our society, is the disintegration of values in our culture. It is the student's inner experience of values that provides the core around which he knows himself as a person, and also gives him something to commit himself to. Back in my college days we found certain values in religion to which we could commit ourselves, economic values in the new socialism, values in pacifism, values in politics, and values in the cause of enlightenment in art, sex, and religion. Unfortunately, the present-day student seems to have only two areas which challenge him in any ultimate sense: international relations in the form of the Peace Corps, and race relations.

What can we do to make the climate on our campuses more nourishing to the growth of values? Certainly we cannot bring back the old values in any external way. But we can help ourselves and our students rediscover the sources of value choices in the accumulated wisdom of man's past. This means, for one thing, a new appreciation of the humanities. When Dean Barzun of Columbia predicts the demise of graduate work in the humanities because the purpose of graduate work has become so overwhelmingly learning how to make a living, and the humanities are techonologized along with the rest of our culture, we must take him seriously; but we can also try to take steps to withstand the trend. I propose that a new understanding of the critical importance of man's *capacity to value* would help rediscover the humanities, not as leisure "hobbies" for indigent elderly ladies, but the very blood and sinew of our value choices which can form these masses of facts into civilization.

What is important in dealing with anxiety is not that teachers give students the *contents* of values, but that students learn the *act of valuing.* Note that I emphasize "value" here as a verb. In the moment of anxiety, whether or not the student will be able to utilize and grow in the experience depends on his own inner capacity to choose his values at that time.

This points, finally, to the matter of *commitment.* Anxiety is used constructively as the person is able to relate to the situation, do his valuing, and then commit himself to a course of action, a way of life. On campuses in this country during the decades until the last one, I noted we were committed to a policy of noncommitment, a questioning of everything merely for the sake of questioning. I believe this has changed, and students now yearn—on quite profound if submerged levels in their personalities—for some attitudes, ways of life about which they can have ultimate concern and to which they can commit themselves. I suspect our students— again on levels that may not be very often articulated—realize that the usually assumed goals of adaptation and survival are not enough, and that Aristotle was right when he said, "Not life, but the good life, is to be valued." Perhaps we are moving into a time (I trust that my hope is not an illusion) when teachers, artists, intellectuals of all sorts, will not be apologetic for committing themselves—when, like Socrates, we shall question courageously because we believe more courageously.

NOTES FOR CHAPTER 3

1. Dwight Macdonald, *Against the American Grain,* Random House, New York, 1962, p. 393.

Part Two

Sources of Anxiety

Since anxiety is the common denominator of the individual's inner experience of these dilemmas, we shall here seek a historical perspective on anxiety. We shall explore the curious triangular relationship between a person's anxiety, his degree of consciousness, and his values.

4

Historical Roots of Modern Anxiety Theories

> To venture causes anxiety, but not to venture is to lose one's self. And to venture in the highest sense is precisely to be conscious of one's self.
>
> —KIERKEGAARD

In America, it has been said, we assume that history begins with the reading of the minutes of the last board meeting. Or more specifically in psychology, history starts with the results of our last experiment.

This antihistorical attitude is an entirely understandable outgrowth of our frontier background, as I shall point out later: every frontiersman did indeed have to start from scratch. But the social sciences seem in particular to lack a dynamic sense of how history molds and forms them and seem especially truncated by the unanalyzed assumption that they sprang, like the fully armored Athena, from the forehead of some nineteenth-century Zeus. And especially has psychology been impoverished by the lack of a dynamic, organic sense of history. For if we do not experience the fact that the people we study, as well as our own methods and our very selves, are products of several thousand years of art, language, exploration, reflection, and other aspects of the emerging human consciousness, we shall have cut ourselves off from our very roots. To cut off history is to sever our arterial link with humanity.

A historical view should help us to see how certain cultural forces and events have shaped and molded the attitudes and behavior patterns which underlie our contemporary psychological conflicts. A historical perspective can also help free us from the ever-present danger—especially a danger in the social sciences—of absolutizing a theory or method which is actually relative to the fact that we live at a given moment in time in the development of our particular culture. Finally, a historical perspective can help us see the common sources of human problems as well as common human goals.

But our task in this chapter is not simply to garner historical facts. We seek, rather, to understand history as a dynamic process which is embodied and operates in the unconscious assumptions of each one of us, just as it operates in the unconscious presuppositions of our culture as a whole. As the genetic experiences of the child are "father to the man," so the patterns which have developed historically in our culture have molded and conditioned each one of us as a member of the society. The patient who comes into a psychotherapist's office or clinic bears with him and embodies in his character structure the historical patterns and influences which have been dominant in the culture. When a patient, for example, endeavors to rationalize his anxiety by ascribing it to this or that intellectually respectable "cause," or when he refuses to admit that the anxiety may have origins beyond the logical "reasons" which he gives, he is behaving not merely according to individual vagary. He is acting as a well-trained child of the modern historical period—a period which, from the time of Descartes in the seventeenth century to our twentieth, has presupposed a dichotomy of reason and emotion.

Thus the individual's anxiety and his ways of meeting it are conditioned by the fact that *he stands at a given point in the development of his culture.* Similarly, the different theories of anxiety, whether presented by Spinoza in the seventeenth century, by Kierkegaard in the nineteenth century, or by Freud in the twentieth century, can be understood only as each theory is seen to be designed to illuminate the anxiety-creating experiences of people at that particular stage in the historical development of the culture. Although foreseen by Dilthey in the nineteenth century, this historical approach has largely been omitted from psychoanalytic investigations. But the exigencies of our historical situation in the twentieth century—the very dilemmas we have discussed—have forced us to realize that a profoundly important aspect of the development of character structure was being overlooked in our investigations. Now that the central importance of the cultural dimension of psychological problems has been admitted on all sides, it may well be that the historical dimension will be the next area to come into its own in our endeavors to understand man's psychological problems.

We shall here, for a few pages, be chiefly concerned with the contributions of philosophers to anxiety theory, since they were the ones who articulated and formulated the meaning of their historical periods. Similar analyses might be made of the economic, religious, or artistic aspects of a historical period. And because of the relative unity of the culture at a given period, I am confident that such analyses from varied approaches would arrive at roughly similar conclusions. I should say also that I do not treat philosophical formulations as either cause or effect, but rather as one expression of the total cultural development of a period. The particular philosophers whose formulations have become important for their own and subsequent centuries are those who succeeded in penetrating and articulating the dominant meaning and direction of the development of their culture. It is in this sense that the formulations made by the intellectual leaders of one century become the common currency, in the form of unconscious assumptions, of large numbers of people in succeeding centuries.

IN THE Middle Ages, the period out of which our modern age was born, the society was collectivist in a normal sense. Each citizen, serf or priest or knight, knew his place in the hierarchy of church and feudalism; and all emotions were channeled in community and religious ceremonies. The accepted values of life were clear, as well as the way to the achievement of these values. "All emotions required a rigid system of conventional forms, for without them passion and ferocity would have made havoc of life." [1] We shall see, oddly enough, that the problems facing us in our day are roughly opposite.

A radical change then occurred with the Renaissance and Reformation in the arrival of a new and enthusiastic belief in the power of the individual, together with a new concrete and empirical concern for physical nature. These changes had as one of their obvious psychological results the increase of the individual's confidence that problems could be overcome by his own courage, by knowledge that he could obtain by his own study and travel, and by following the guidance of his own conscience in religious and ethical matters. As a young man, Descartes, for example, set out to travel somewhat as nowadays we embark on a Ph.D. program. The method which became the tool of the new devotion to knowledge and individual reason was mathematics, Arabic mathematics having been borrowed from the Mohammedans and introduced into western Europe via Spain in the thirteenth century. The understanding and control of physical nature then became Western man's dominant and enthusiastic concern. This enterprise was greatly expedited by Descartes' dichotomy between mind and body, with its corollary that the body and physical nature could be understood by mathematical, mechanical laws.

In the late Renaissance, that is, in the sixteenth century, there are several writers who, though unfortunately rarely studied in connection with modern psychological developments, presented germinal ideas for the modern period. One is Giordano Bruno (later to be burned at the stake by the Inquisition) whose idea of Creation as concentric circles with the self at the center gave the original philosophical orientation for modernism. Another is Jakob Boehme, a German mystic and precursor of Protestant thought who wrote with amazing insight about the relation between anxiety and individual creative effort. And a third is Paracelsus, a physician in the Renaissance who emphasized the influence of the patient's own will and decision in the achievement of health. It is with Paracelsus, according to Tillich, that the physician began to take over in modern culture the role which the priest had played in medievalism.

The guiding intellectual principle of this cultural revolution, which, beginning in the Renaissance, resulted in the overthrow of feudalism and absolutism and led finally to the supremacy of the bourgeoisie, was the belief in the *rational capacities of the individual*. This is termed the confidence in "autonomous reason" by Tillich and in Cassirer's term, "mathematical reason," since mathematics was conceived as the chief tool of reason. In contrast to medieval collectivism, it was emphasized in the fifteenth and sixteenth centuries that each man was a rational individual who could arrive at autonomy in his intellectual, economic, religious, and emotional life. In the seventeenth century, following the Renaissance, this emergent emphasis on individual reason received its philosophical formulation by Descartes, Spinoza, Leibniz and others. This century, which in its group of powerful and seminal thinkers also included Locke, Galileo, and Newton, produced the ideas which were to dominate most of the modern period up to our time.

The "father of modern philosophy," Descartes, was particularly interesting in that he made individual reason the basis for the psychological identity of the self in his famous principle, "I think, therefore I am." Legend has it that Descartes crawled into his stove one morning, determined to work out a basic concept for his philosophy, and emerged at evening with the above principle. This legend is a graphic symbol for the individual isolation which was always one aspect of the rationalism bequeathed to us from the seventeenth century. We can see the individualistic implications of Descartes' contention that the thinking function is the basis of identity by comparing it to our twentieth century concept that *the self becomes aware of its identity in a social context:* e.g., the child finds that it is a self when it sees itself in relation to and differentiated from the other persons in its family.

Descartes made a sharp distinction between mind and the processes of thought, on one hand, and body on the other. Thought has *intention,* as he put it, and the body and nature have *extension.* This dichotomy plagued us in late centuries, and was to be a focal point for the problem of anxiety. At the time, however, the chief consequence of Descartes' dichotomy was its corollary that the body, like all of physical nature, was understandable and controllable by mechanical, mathematical laws. The way was paved for the increasing preoccupation in modern times with phenomena that were susceptible to mathematical and mechanical treatment, and for the increasing suppression of nonmechanical and so-called "irrational" experience. This suppression of everything which was not mechanical went hand in hand, both as cause and effect, with the needs of the new industrialism following the Renaissance. For what could be calculated and measured had practical utility in the industrial workaday world, and what was irrational did not.

Now the confidence that the body and physical nature were mathematically controllable did have far-reaching anxiety-dispelling effects. It gave hope for overcoming the actual threats of physical nature, as well as promise of vast expansion of man's capacities to meet his material needs. Both of these promises were later to be thoroughly justified by great progress in the physical sciences and in industrialism. In addition, a way was opened for *freeing man from irrational fears, for dissolving the multitudes of fears of devils, sorcerers, and forms of magic* which had been the foci of pervasive anxiety in the last two centuries of the Middle Ages as well as in the Renaissance itself. As Professor Tillich has phrased it, the Cartesians, by means of their assumption that the soul could not influence the body, were able to "disenchant the world." One example of this is that the persecution of witches, which had occurred through the Renaissance up until the early eighteenth century, was overcome through Cartesian formulations.

Spinoza took the final step in the seventeenth century: he sought *to make the human emotions controllable through mathematical reason.* Thus he presented us with an ethics in the form of geometry. We shall not endeavor to summarize Spinoza's astute psychological insights, although we may note that he did anticipate almost word for word some later psychoanalytic and psychosomatic concepts. Instead we shall consider only his belief that fear could be overcome by the correct use of reason. Fear, he believed, is essentially a subjective problem: "I saw that all the things I feared, and which feared me had nothing good or bad in them save insofar as the mind was affected by them." [2] He held that fear and hope always go together: "Fear cannot be without hope, nor hope without fear." [3] Both these affects are characteristic of the person in doubt (i.e., the person who has not learned the right use of reason). Fear, he wrote, "arises from a weakness of mind and therefore does not appertain to the use of reason. . . . Therefore [he concluded] the more we endeavor to live under the guidance of reason, the less we endeavor to depend on hope, and the more to deliver ourselves and make ourselves free from fear and overcome fortune as much as possible, and finally to direct our actions by the certain advice of reason." [4] Spinoza's guidance on how to overcome fear was consistent with the general rational emphasis of the time: emotions are not repressed, but rather are made amenable to reason. It is true, he held, that one emotion can be overcome only by a contrary, stronger emotion, but this can be accomplished by paying attention to the "ordering of our thoughts and images. . . . We must think of courage in the same manner in order to lay aside fear, that is, we must enumerate and imagine the common perils of life and in what manner they may best be avoided and overcome by courage." [5]

It is the term "certain" which leaps out of us from Spinoza's writing on fear; the removal of doubt, hope and fear is possible if we direct ourselves by the *certain* advice of reason. It is obvious that if one believed, as Spinoza in his century could believe, that such intellectual and emotional certainty could be achieved—if you could, for example, be as certain about an ethical problem as about a proposition in geometry—untold psychological security would result. Such a faith may seem very appealing but scarcely attainable to citizens of the anxiety-ridden twentieth century. To understand Spinoza's confidence, therefore, we must recall that the expanding cultural climate of his seventeenth century was radically different from that of Kierkegaard, Kafka, and Freud in the subsequent nineteenth and twentieth centuries.

Another reason Spinoza could have such confidence was that the broad and profound ethical and religious base of his thinking saved him from the dichotomies of the contemporary seventeenth-century rationalism. But Spinoza speaks of fear, not anxiety. His analysis stands only on the threshold of the problem of anxiety. He points toward anxiety at times, as when he sets hope in juxtaposition to fear, but he does not cross the threshold. He seems to have been able to meet his problems on the level of fear, and hence the central problem of anxiety did not intrude itself into his thought. We conclude that, given the cultural situation in which he lived, Spinoza's confidence in reason served him satisfactorily.

BUT ANOTHER and dissenting voice speaks out of the seventeenth century, that of Blaise Pascal. Though like his contemporary intellectual leaders in his mathematical and scientific genius, Pascal was exceptional in that he did not share the prevalent confidence in individual reason and in that he directly experienced the problem of anxiety. He did not believe that human nature, in all its variety and contradiction, could be comprehended by mathematical reason, nor that rational certitude was possible in the field of man's emotions in any sense similar to the certitude of geometry and physics. He questioned the prevailing confidence in reason because it failed to take sufficiently into account the power of the emotions. His classic sentence, "The heart has reasons which the reason knows not of," is an admirable phrasing of the problem for Freud and psychoanalysis two centuries later. Pascal had a tremendous respect for reason, and indeed believed it to be the basis of morality, but he pointed out that reason in the individual is in actual practice pliable to every sense. And reason is very frequently used in rationalization for vanity, special interest, and injustice.

Pascal was directly concerned with anxiety, not only anxiety which he himself experienced but also that which he believed he observed in his fellowmen. He cited as evidence the "perpetual restlessness in which men pass their lives," [6] and the fact of people's unceasing efforts through diversions to escape from "thoughts of themselves." He connected anxiety with the precarious, contingent situation of man. Pascal, indeed, knew a great deal about the human dilemma. This is why his words often sound so eloquently modern, and speak so directly to our condition.

We have submitted that the confidence in reason, as interpreted by intellectual leaders of the seventeenth century, served to dispel anxiety. It is some support for this thesis that Pascal, the one who could not share this confidence—the one, in fact, who had not really absorbed the Renaissance confidence in the individual—should be the one who at the same time could not avoid anxiety.

Despite Pascal's rebuttal, the confidence in individual reason won out and served as a central, unifying concept in the seventeenth and eighteenth centuries. The problem in our historical inquiry now becomes, How were these thinkers able to overcome the tendencies toward *psychological isolation inherent in the individualistic nature of this reason?* If Descartes, as a spokesman for his age, finds his personal identity in the fact that he, as an individual shut up in his stove, is able to think, how is he to make the bridge to his community? How is he able to escape profound feelings of isolation and consequent anxiety? If Leibniz makes his basic concept, the monad, a discrete reality with no communication with other monads, how is he and how is the age for which he speaks able to escape a feeling of basic individual separation? In actual fact, feelings of isolation were widespread in the individualism emerging in the Renaissance. This problem had to be solved if psychological community was to be achieved and the ever-present threat of anxiety to be dispelled.

A clear answer to this problem was given in seventeenth century thought by the belief in preestablished harmony. In its economic form, this was the belief that if each man pursued his own individual economic motives, strove competitively for his own economic gain, his striving would at the same time redound to the benefit of his social group. This was the famous *laissez-faire* concept of economics. On the psychological level, it was believed that the free pursuit of individual reason would automatically lead to a harmony of the individual's conclusions with those of his fellowmen and hence to a harmony of the individual with society. On the philosophical level, Leibniz put it most clearly in his assertion that each monad was in preestablished harmony with other monads and with universal reality. Thus in theory the man who courageously pursued individual reason need not feel isolated and thereby anxious. This theory was a sound reflection of the cultural state of the seventeenth and eighteenth centuries; *laissez-faire* individual economic striving, for example, in the expanding stages of capitalism *did* tremendously increase the capacity for meeting the material needs of everyone. There was amazing, far-reaching progress in science, in the spread of knowledge and in the broadening of the base of individual political rights, attending this belief in individual reason and its harmonistic corollaries.

Given the cultural milieu in which Spinoza, Leibniz, and the others lived and taught, it seems that their confidence in individual reason did serve them satisfactorily. For that was a time—roughly parallel to the fifth century in ancient Greece—when the culture was moving toward unity in its basic symbols. Thus the citizens found in their society, and particularly in religion and education, more psychological support.

BUT A GROWING disunity began to rumble in the middle and second half of the nineteenth century, and then became apparent and much more extensive in the twentieth century.[7] This disunity went hand in hand with the great progress which had been made in the application of mathematical reason and mechanical laws to physical nature. The far-reaching achievement of the physical sciences, with the promise of making Nature man's servant, together with the vast progress of industrialism and its promise of meeting human physical needs, gave ample support for the great confidence which had been placed in the endeavor to understand and control Nature by mechanical laws. By the nineteenth century the earlier confidence in individual reason as related to all aspects of life had changed to an *emphasis on techniques* and the application of reason more and more exclusively to technical problems.

Thus in the nineteenth century the belief in autonomous reason, with its corollary confidence in automatic harmony, began to break down. The prophetic thinkers of that century—Kierkegaard, Nietzsche, and Marx, for instance—saw this occurring and described the fissures in contemporary cultural which were later to generate widespread anxiety. Marx pointed out that while individual economic striving had increased social weal during the expanding stages of industrialism, it now served a contrary purpose in the stage of monopoly capitalism and actually made for the *alienation* and *dehumanization* of man. Nietzsche warned of science becoming a "factory" and he feared nihilistic consequences. This nineteenth century was characterized by Cassirer as the era of "autonomous sciences." A unifying principle was lacking. "Each individual thinker gives us his own picture of human nature," was Cassirer's comment on the nineteenth century, and whereas each picture is based on empirical evidence, each "theory becomes a Procrustean bed on which empirical facts are stretched to fit a preconceived pattern." [8] Cassirer believed this antagonism of ideas constituted a grave "threat to the whole extent of our ethical and cultural life." [9]

The increasing disunity and compartmentalization in nineteenth century culture can be seen clearly on the psychological side. It lay in the tendency to see man as consisting of different "faculties"— e.g., reason, emotion, and will power. Our nineteenth-century man was supposed, like a successful businessman or industrialist, to make decisions by practical reason and then to enforce these decisions by his strong will power. So we see this citizen of the nineteenth century *trying to solve his personal psychological problems by the same methods as had been so effective in mastering physical nature and so successful in the industrial world.* The dichotomy of mind and body of the seventeenth century now took the form of a radical separation of reason and emotion, with voluntaristic effort (will) enthroned as the agent of decision—and this generally resulted in the denial of the emotions. The seventeenth-century belief in the *rational control* of the emotions now became *the habit of repressing* the emotions.

This cultural and psychological disunity was to produce inner disunity and trauma, and therefore anxiety, in vast numbers of people in the twentieth century. It also specifically set the twofold problem of anxiety for Kierkegaard and Freud: How is the dichotomy of reason and emotion to be overcome, and how can the isolated individual achieve community with his fellows?

Thus Freud and Kierkegaard, like Nietzsche and Schopenhauer, sought in different ways to rediscover the repressed dynamic, unconscious, so-called "irrational" springs of man's behavior, and to unite these with man's rational functions. It is only against the background of nineteenth-century compartmentalization of personality that Freud's discoveries relating to the unconscious, and his techniques designed to assist the individual to a new unity, can be understood. Likewise, against this historical background, we can understand Freud's strictures against the academic psychology and academic medicine of his day—both disciplines which were preoccupied with the elements of behavior that could be isolated, tabulated and measured according to the traditional methods of mathematical rationalism. These strictures were not the expression merely of Freud's prejudice or distemper, but represented a real issue, namely, the urgent necessity of overcoming the dichotomy between reason and emotion.

Since Freud's work itself does not properly fall into a study of historical roots, we now turn to that astounding genius of the middle of the last century, Sören Kierkegaard. Kierkegaard has been recognized in this country only in the last two decades, whereas he has been known in Europe for half a century as one of the great psychologists of all time.

Kierkegaard's little book *The Concept of Anxiety* was first published in 1844.[10] We have only to compare Kierkegaard with Spinoza to appreciate how different was the cultural climate of the nineteenth century from that of the seventeenth. Spinoza and Kierkegaard both had broad ethical and religious bases for their thought, and both were remarkably gifted with psychological insight and intuition. But whereas Spinoza in his time sought, with considerable success, rational certitude in the form of geometric proofs in his dealing with fear, Kierkegaard wrote in his day, "in the same degree that the excellence of the proof increases, certitude seems to decrease." He who "has observed the contemporary generation will surely not deny that the incongruity in it and the reason for its anxiety and restlessness is this, that in one direction truth increases in extent, in mass, partly also in abstract clarity, whereas certitude steadily decreases." [11] Certitude, he believed, was an inner quality of integrity attainable only by the individual who could think, feel, and act as a psychological and ethical unity.

Kierkegaard emphatically rejected traditional rationalism as artificial. He vehemently argued that Hegel's system, which identified abstract thought with reality, was a way of tricking men into an avoidance of the reality of their human situation. "Away from speculation," he cried, "away from 'the system' and back to reality!" [12] He insisted that thinking cannot be divorced from feeling and willing, that "truth exists for the particular individual only as he himself produces it in action." [13] That is to say, reality can be approached and experienced only by the whole individual as a feeling and acting as well as a thinking organism. Thus, in a way somewhat similar to that of Schelling, Nietzsche, and even Feuerbach and Marx on the sociological side, Kierkegaard sought to overcome the dichotomy of reason and emotion by turning men's attentions to the reality of immediate experience which underlies both subjectivity and objectivity.

Specifically attacking the problem of anxiety, Kierkegaard noted that we escape neurotic anxiety to the extent that we become free as individuals and at the same time achieve community with our fellows. For him individual freedom was to be radically distinguished from mere *freedom from* restrictions and objections, which had been a dominant conception of freedom since the Renaissance, and even more was to be distinguished from the vacuous, mechanical, pseudo-freedom of the typical participant in our modern bourgeois commercial and industrial routines.

For Kierkegaard freedom meant an expansion of self-awareness and of the capacity to act responsibly as a self. It meant an ever-increasing capacity to confront our possibilities, both in individual development and in deepening relations with our fellows, together with an actualizing of these possibilities. This achieving of possibilities is a continual venturing into new areas, as seen most simply in the case of the growing child. Hence Kierkegaard held that *freedom always involves potential anxiety.* Anxiety, as he puts it epigrammatically, is "the dizziness of freedom." We should emphasize that Kierkegaard thought of this anxiety as "normal," not "neurotic"; his concept was a forerunner of what Otto Rank later described as the anxiety inherent in individuation and what Kurt Goldstein described as the normal anxiety in the individual's meeting the inescapable shocks of growth and experience. An essential element in understanding human anxiety is that man's range of possibility of development is so much greater than that of animals.[14] The greater the potential freedom of the individual, Kierkegaard held, or as we could phrase it from another side, the more creative possibilities the individual man has, the greater is his potential anxiety.

But a distinct characteristic of man is his capacity for *awareness* of his own possibilities. This brings Kierkegaard to his important concept of the relation of *conflict* to anxiety. The anxiety of the very young child he believed was "ambiguous," "unreflective"; the child is not aware of the separation between himself and his environment. But with the development of self-awareness in the child—what is meant in some circles, though I feel inadequately described, by the development of the ego and superego functions—conscious choice enters the picture. The child becomes aware that his aims and desires may involve clashes with parents and defiance of them. Individuation (becoming a self) is now gained only at the price of confronting the anxiety inherent in taking a stand *against* as well as *with* one's environment. Self-awareness makes possible self-directed individual development. This self-awareness is the basis in the growing individual for responsibility, inner conflict, and guilt feeling.

We do not have space to go into Kierkegaard's penetrating and fruitful, though difficult and perhaps controversial, treatment of conflict, creativity, and guilt. Suffice it to say that he believed inner conflict and guilt feeling are always a concomitant of creativity. These are not to be termed neurotic, nor do they result in neurotic anxiety so long as the individual can confront his creative crises and resolve them for further expansion of the self. For example, every creative possibility in individual development involves some killing of the past, some breaking of past forms or patterns; to move ahead raises the unavoidable spectre of isolation from one's fellows and one's previous patterns; one is tempted to remain in the familiar and the safe, not to venture. But one achieves selfhood only by moving ahead, despite conflict, guilt, isolation and anxiety. If one does not move ahead, the result is ultimately *neurotic anxiety*.

For Kierkegaard, neurotic anxiety is the result of *retrenchment*, which occurs because the person is afraid of freedom. This retrenchment involves blocking off areas of freedom of experience or awareness. Here we have an early statement of the process that was later to be called "repression" by Freud and "dissociation" by Sullivan. Like these two later students of man, Kierkegaard believed that when we try to avoid confronting a "real" fear or an experience involving "normal anxiety," we engage in a blocking off of awareness and experience, with neurotic anxiety as a later consequence. Kierkegaard's apt term for neurosis was *shut-upness*. The shut-up person is not shut up *with* himself, but *from* himself, as well as from others. This personality is characterized by various forms of rigidity, unfreedom, vacuousness, and tediousness.

The shut-up person lacks communicativeness, whereas "freedom," Kierkegaard wrote, "is continually communicating." Thus the concentric circles of the widening and deepening self involve at the same time expanding circles of meaningful relations with one's fellowmen. He believed the two sources of neurotic anxiety—disunity within the self and lack of accord with one's fellows—are overcome by simultaneous processes; to overcome one is to overcome the other at the same time. But neither can be achieved unless the individual has the courage to confront and move through the threatening experiences of isolation and anxiety which are "normal" in the sense that they cannot be avoided if one is to fulfill one's possibilities in the achieving of selfhood. It is thus understandable that Kierkegaard regarded anxiety as a teacher; in fact, he held anxiety is a better teacher than reality, for reality can be temporarily avoided whereas anxiety is an ever-present educator you carry within yourself.

IN THIS CHAPTER—if I may be permitted such an academic gesture as offering a summary—I have traced briefly two problems in our historical exploration: the dichotomy of reason and emotion, and the isolation of the individual from his community. I have pointed out that these problems were and are fundamental to the problem of anxiety in the modern period. I have indicated how these problems were met, and how the anxiety inherent in them was, to a considerable extent, dispelled during the major part of the modern period since the Renaissance by various forms of the belief that if the individual energetically pursued his own economic gain and his own reason, automatic harmony with his fellowmen and his metaphysical world would result. I have described how this belief lost its efficacy in the nineteenth century, when individual reason became intellectualistic repression and *laissez-faire* economics became a rationalization for dehumanization and mechanization of the individual.

In conclusion I can only suggest how these problems are related to the problem of anxiety in the twentieth century. First, I wish to submit a hypothesis, namely, that when the presuppositions, the unconscious assumptions of values, in a society are generally accepted, the individual can meet threats on the basis of these presuppositions. He then reacts to threats with fear, not anxiety. But when the presuppositions in a society are themselves threatened, the individual has no basis on which to orient himself when he is confronted with a specific threat. Since *the inner citadel of society itself is in a state of confusion and traumatic change during such periods,* the individual has no solid ground on which to meet the specific threats which confront him. The result for the individual is profound disorientation, psychological confusion, and hence chronic or acute panic and anxiety. Now is this not the state of our culture in the twentieth century? It is my belief, in other words, that the disintegration of the presuppositions of our historical culture which I have pointed to in this chapter, is intimately related to the widespread anxiety in the twentieth century. And it is also related to the particular difficulties of the human dilemma we must confront in our time.

In such a period, when society no longer provides the individual with adequate psychological and ethical orientation, he is forced, often in desperation, to look deeply within himself to discover a new basis for orientation and integration. It is this need which called forth psychoanalysis and the new dynamic psychology; indeed, the aiding of the individual to discover a new unity within himself is the great contribution of psychology since Freud. The meeting of this need of modern man to find his meaning within himself is also what called forth the development of existentialism.

But with respect to the other and broader problem—the construction of new forms of psychological and ethical community, so that the individual may be meaningfully related to his fellowmen in creative work and in love—our task has only begun. I believe that the meeting of this challenge, and thus the overcoming of a prime source of anxiety, requires the combined work not only of psychologists and psychopathologists but also of workers in all fields of social science and in religion, philosophy and the arts as well. I have said that in periods when the values of a culture have unity and cogency, the citizen has means of meeting and coping with his anxiety. When the values are in disunity, the individual, feeling himself without moorings, tends to evade and repress his normal anxiety. He thereby sets the stage for his developing neurotic anxiety. Thus values and anxiety are very closely interrelated. To this we shall now turn.

NOTES FOR CHAPTER 4

1. Johan Huizinga, *The Waning of the Middle Ages,* New York, 1924, p. 40.
2. "Treatise on the Correction of the Understanding," in *Spinoza's Ethics,* Everyman edition, London, 1910, p. 227.
3. "Origin and Nature of the Emotions," *ibid.,* p. 131.
4. "The Strength of the Emotions," *ibid.,* p. 175.
5. "Power of the Intellect," *ibid.,* p. 208.
6. *Pascal's Thoughts,* translated by Craig, Carter, New York, 1825, p. 110.
7. I have described this in some detail in my book *The Meaning of Anxiety* (1950).
8. Cassirer, Ernst, *An Essay on Man,* Yale University Press, New Haven, 1944, p. 21.
9. *Ibid.,* p. 22.
10. Translated into English by Walter Lowrie, and published under the title *The Concept of Dread,* Princeton, 1944.
11. *Ibid.,* p. 124.
12. Lowrie, Walter, *A Short Life of Kierkegaard,* Princeton, 1944, p. 116.
13. *Concept of Dread,* p. 123.
14. Cf. the biologist Portmann's description of the freedom of movement of man in relation to his world—the "world openness" of man —touched on in Chapter 1 above.

5

Anxiety and Values

> *No people can live without valuing. Valuing is creating;*
> *hear it ye creative ones! Without valuation the nut of*
> *existence is hollow. Hear it, ye creative ones!*
>
> —NIETZSCHE

The distinctive quality of human anxiety arises from the fact that man is the valuing animal, the being who interprets his life and world in terms of symbols and meanings, and identifies these with his existence as a self. This we shall explore in this chapter. As Nietzsche remarked, "Man should be named the 'valuator'." It is the threat to these values that causes anxiety. Indeed, I define anxiety as *the apprehension cued off by a threat to some value which the individual holds essential to his existence as a self.* The threat may be to physical life itself, i.e., death; or to psychological life, i.e., loss of freedom. Or it may be to some value the person identifies with his existence as a self: patriotism, the love of a special person, prestige among one's peers, devotion to scientific truth or to religious belief.

A classic and dramatic illustration of this is seen in the remark of the unsophisticated Tom, whom Wolf and Wolff [1] studied for several months in their significant work on anxiety and gastric functions at New York Hospital. Readers of the report will recall that Tom and his wife lay awake all one night worrying whether Tom's job in the hospital laboratory would last or whether he would have to go back on government relief. The next morning the gastric readings for Tom's anxiety were the highest of any encountered in all those studies. The significant point, to the doctors, is Tom's remark "If I couldn't support my family, I'd as soon jump off the end of the dock." The threat which underlay this great anxiety in Tom was thus not that of physical deprivation—he and his family could have got along on relief—but was rather a threat to a status which Tom, like so many men in our society, held even more important than life: the ability to fulfill one's role as a middle-class provider for one's family. The loss of this status would be tantamount to not existing as a person.

We see similar examples in the area of sex. Sex gratification in itself, of course, is a value. But at every turn in dealing with patients in psychotherapy one notes that the physical gratification itself is only a small part of the question, since a person will be thrown into conflict and anxiety when rejected sexually by one partner but not by another. Obviously other elements—prestige, tenderness, personal understanding—give the sexual experience with one partner a value the other does not have. It is fair to say, incidentally, that the less mature the person, the more the simply physiological gratification itself carries the value and the less difference is made by *who* gives the gratification; whereas the more mature and differentiated the person, the more such other factors as tenderness and the personal relationship to the other person determine the value of the sexual experience.

Death is the most obvious threat cueing off anxiety, for unless one holds beliefs in immortality which are not common in our culture, death stands for the ultimate blotting out of one's existence as a self. But immediately we note a very curious fact: some people *prefer to die rather than to surrender some other value*. The taking away of psychological and spiritual freedom was not infrequently a greater threat than death itself to persons under the dictatorships of Europe. "Give me liberty or give me death" is not necessarily histrionic or evidence of a neurotic attitude. Indeed, there is reason for believing, as we shall observe later, that it may represent the most mature form of *distinctively human* behavior. Nietzsche, Jaspers, and others of the more profound existentialists, in fact, have pointed out that physical life itself is not fully satisfying and meaningful until one can consciously choose another value which he holds more dear than life itself.

What is the origin of these values, the threat to which results in anxiety? Obviously, the infant's first value is the care, nourishment, and love it receives from its mother or parental substitutes; a threat to these, being indeed a threat to the infant's existence, gives rise to profound anxiety. But as maturation proceeds, the values are transformed. They become desire for approval by mother, for example, then "success" in the eyes of parents or peers, and later on, status in cultural terms; and ultimately in the mature adult the values may become devotion to freedom, to a religious belief, or to scientific truth. I do not propose this as an exact maturation scale; I mean only to illustrate roughly that maturation involves a continuous transformation of the original values identified with one's existence, the threat to which causes anxiety; and that in the normal human being these values take on an increasingly symbolic character.

It is an error to think of these later values as *merely the extension* of the original value of preserving mother's care and love, or to think that all values are merely different guises of the meeting of primary needs. Capacities emerge in the developing person which render him a *new* gestalt; on the pattern of emergent evolution, the maturing person continually develops new capacities out of the old, new symbols, values in a new form. To be sure, the more an individual's anxiety is neurotic, the more he is probably trying to satisfy year after year the same values he held at earlier stages: he still, as we know in so many clinical cases, repetitiously and compulsively seeks mother's love and care. But the healthier the person, the less his values as an adult can be comprehended as a sum of his previous needs and instincts.

The most important emergent capacity in the human being is self-relatedness. It begins somewhere after the first few months and probably is fairly well developed in the child by the age of two. Thereafter, the values of love and care take on a new character: they are not simply something *received,* but are reacted to by the child with some degree of self-awareness. He may now *accept* the mother's care, *defy* it, *use* it for various forms of power demands or what not. A patient at a clinic reported that he had learned at an early age to put his hands against the wall and push his high chair over so that his parents would catch it. The value involved here was not self-preservation, that is, being saved from hitting the floor (he had his parents so well trained that this contingency never arose). The value gained was rather the satisfaction and security involved in his power to force his parents to sit on pins and needles, ready to jump to his aid.

We can see how the value of love also develops a new characteristic when we observe that in the mature person—the adult with a degree of autonomy—some choice, some conscious affirmation, some self-aware participation, is necessary in loving and accepting love if the experience of love is to yield full satisfaction. The value then lies in being able to give to the other person as well as to receive. Such a mature individual may well experience his most severe anxiety if his opportunity to give love to the partner is threatened.

Thus, in understanding the origin of values—the threats to which, as we have seen, cause anxiety—we must avoid two errors. The first is the error of not relating the value to the early needs for love and care. But the second error is thinking that the matter is *just* that and overlooking the fact that emergent qualities in the person make the value threatened at each stage of development genuinely new.

LET US LOOK now at this distinctive capacity for self-relatedness of the human being, a capacity which is crucially significant for understanding human anxiety. It is man's capacity to stand outside himself, to know he is the subject as well as the object of experience, to see himself as the entity who is acting in the world of objects.[2] This unique quality which distinguishes man from the rest of nature has been described, as we indicated earlier, in various ways by Goldstein, and others. In his early work, Hobart Mowrer, following Korzybski, calls it the human being's time-binding quality: "the capacity to bring the past into the present as a part of the total causal nexus in which living organisms behave (act and react) is the essence of 'mind' and 'personality' alike." Howard Liddell informs us that his sheep can keep time for about ten minutes, his dogs for about half an hour. But the human being can keep time into the distant future—he can plan for decades or centuries; and we should add, he can worry about this future and suffer anxiety in anticipating his own eventual death. It makes us the historical mammals who can "look before and after, and pine for what is not." By understanding the past, we can mold and to some small extent influence the future. Neurosis, as Lawrence Kubie has indicated, has its source in the distortion of these symbolic functions as a result of a dichotomy between conscious and unconscious processes which starts early in the development of each human infant.

It was Adolf Meyer, so Sullivan suggests, who held that the human being operates on a hierarchy of organization, and that the physiological functions should be seen as subordinated to the integrating functions and particularly to man's capacity to use symbols as tools.[3] What is important here for understanding anxiety is that man, the symbol-user, interprets his experience in symbolic terms and holds these symbols as values, the threats to which give rise to profound anxiety. The understanding of anxiety can thus never be separated from ethical symbols, which are one aspect of the human being's normal milieu. Through his distinctive social capacity to see himself as others see him, to imagine himself empathetically in his fellowman's or a stranger's position, the person can direct his decisions in the light of long-term values, which are the basis of ethics and therefore the basis of moral anxiety.

I use the terms "symbols" and "values" incidentally, in the sense of the *quintessence* of experience. They are a "boiling down" of the most real relationships and satisfactions; and thus a threat to a symbolic value, like the flag or Tom's status, can have tremendous anxiety-arousing power.

An individual's values and his anxiety, we saw in the last chapter, are conditioned by the fact that he lives in a given culture at a particular moment in the historical development of that culture. This is by no means just because the person happened to grow up among others and therefore reflects their opinions, but because it is the essence of man's nature to interpret his values in the context of his relation to other people and their expectations. Tom, who believed he had to be a self-supporting middle-class male, was validating himself by values that have been dominant in Western society since the Renaissance. As Fromm and Kardiner and others long ago made clear, the dominant value since then has been competitive prestige measured in terms of work and financial success. If you achieved this, you felt yourself a person and your anxiety was allayed; if you did not, you were subject to powerful anxiety, and you lost your sense of being a self.

A curious fact, however, has emerged in the last two decades: this dominant competitive value has apparently been reversed. David Riesman tells us in *The Lonely Crowd* that young people rarely have the goal of competitive success any more; they want not to be first in school but rather to stay somewhere in the upper middle. Lo and behold, the dominant value then becomes not getting ahead of the next man but being like everyone else—that is, conformity. One then validates himself by fitting into the herd; what makes you prey to anxiety is to be different, to stand out. This development has been part of the special problems in recent decades of anti-intellectualism, witch-hunts, suspicion of the original and creative person, and the general tendency to avoid anxiety by assuming protective coloring.

We come now to the special form of anxiety called loneliness. Freud, Rank, and others have suggested that all anxiety may be, at bottom, separation anxiety. And thus loneliness—the awareness of separation—may well turn out to be the most painful *conscious* and *immediate* form of anxiety. The cultural values of conformity, the adjustment of the "radar type" who reflects his signals from the crowd around him, are related to the prevalence of loneliness in our day, about which Sullivan and Fromm-Reichmann have enlightenedly written. Loneliness is a common experience of those who conform, for while on one hand they are driven to conform because of loneliness, on the other, the validating of the self by means of becoming like everyone else reduces their sense of self and their experience of personal identity. The process makes for inner emptiness, thus causing greater loneliness.

Shall we say that in this shift from competition to conformity, the dominant value and hence the locus for the genesis of anxiety, since the Renaissance, has changed? Yes, in part. Certainly one of the clearest reasons for the prevalence of anxiety in our culture is the fact that we live in a time when almost all social values are in radical change, when one world is dying and the new one is not yet born.

But is there not a more specific explanation which underlies *both* the value of competitive success, dominant from the Renaissance until recently, and its apparent present opposite, conformity? Do not both arise from one cause, namely, *modern Western man's disruption in his relationship to nature?* Since the Renaissance, Western man has been infatuated with the goal of gaining power over nature. He has transformed the broad concept of reason of the seventeenth and eighteenth centuries into technical reason in the nineteenth and twentieth centuries, and he has dedicated himself to the exploitation of nature. Ever since Descartes' dichotomy in the seventeenth century between subjective experience and the objective world, Western man has progressively sought to see nature as entirely separated from him, and he has thought he could best study nature, and "conquer" it, by making it entirely objective and impersonal.

The deep loneliness and isolation this entailed was already sensed in the seventeenth century by Pascal, who said, "When I consider the brief span of my life, swallowed up in the eternity before and behind it, the small space that I fill or even see, engulfed in the infinite immensity of spaces which I know not, and which know not me, I am afraid and wonder to see myself here rather than there; for there is no reason why I should be here rather than there, now rather than then."

Since modern men were *successful* in validating themselves by power *over* nature for several centuries, the loneliness and isolation inherent in this situation became widespread only in our twentieth century. Particularly with the advent of the atom bomb, sensitive laymen as well as scientists began to experience the loneliness of being strangers in the universe; and it has made many Western men, like Pascal, afraid. Our contemporaneous loneliness and anxiety thus go deeper than alienation from the natural world.

But what about *human* nature, also a part of nature? The answer is that the methods which were so magnificently successful in measuring and harnessing inanimate nature were, in the nineteenth century, applied to human nature. We conceived of ourselves as objects to be weighed and measured and analyzed. And we could not escape, then, seeing ourselves like inanimate nature as *impersonal*. Human nature became something to gain power over, to manipulate, and to exploit—as we exploit the coal in our mountains and the steel we hammer into bodies for our automobiles.

So modern man was set up in an undeclared war upon himself. "Conquering ourselves" of the Victorian nineteenth century became "manipulating ourselves" in the twentieth. The human dilemma of subject relating to object, which we described in our first chapter, became perverted into the subject, "I," exploiting the rest of myself, the impersonal object "It". This sets up a vicious circle—one of the outcomes of which is the overflowing of our psychological clinics. The vicious circle can find relief, so long as it remains within this deteriorated form of the dilemma, only in the diminishing of the subject, that is, the reduction of consciousness. But alas! we cannot in the long run expect healing to come from applying more of the same disease we seek to cure.

Several straws in the wind show movements in our society toward recovering an indigenous relation with nature. Modern physics is one such movement. As Werner Heisenberg says, the essence of modern physics is that the Copernican view that nature is to be studied "out there," entirely separate from man, is no longer tenable; nature cannot be understood apart from man's subjective involvement, and vice versa.[4] The West's new interest in Eastern thought, in its healthy aspects, points in the same direction. Oriental thought never suffered our radical split between subject and object, between I-the-person and the world "out there," and therefore escaped the special Western brand of separation from nature and consequent loneliness.[5] In any event, we cannot understand modern Western man's anxiety except as we see him in his historical "bind" as the heir of several centuries of radical splitting of subject and object with its consequent disrupted relation with nature.

Since anxiety is the reaction to a threat to values one identified with his existence, no one can escape anxiety, for no values are unassailable. This is the inevitable normal anxiety. Furthermore, values are always in process of change and reformation. The only apparent escape—albeit a self-defeating one—from the anxiety that occurs in an age of transformation of values is to crystallize one's values into dogma. And dogma, whether of the religious or scientific variety, is a temporary security bought at the price of surrendering one's opportunity for fresh learning and new growth. Dogma leads to neurotic anxiety.

WE MUST NOW differentiate neurotic from normal anxiety, for without a concept of normal anxiety we are unable to discern the neurotic form. *Normal* anxiety is anxiety which is proportionate to the threat, does not involve repression, and can be confronted constructively on the conscious level (or can be relieved if the objective situation is altered). *Neurotic* anxiety, on the other hand, is a reaction which is disproportionate to the threat, involves repression and other forms of intrapsychic conflict, and is managed by various kinds of blocking-off of activity and awareness. The anxiety connected with the "loneliness at the top" and the "loneliness of the long distance runner" which the movies tell us about can be seen as *normal* anxiety. The anxiety that comes from conforming, to escape this loneliness, is the *neurotic* transformation of the original normal anxiety.

Actually, neurotic anxiety develops when a person has been unable to meet normal anxiety at the time of the actual crisis in his growth and the threat to his values. Neurotic anxiety is the end result of previously unmet normal anxiety.

Normal anxiety is most obvious in the steps in individuation which occur at every stage in one's development. The child learns to walk and leaves the past security of the playpen; he goes off to school; at adolescence he reaches out toward the opposite sex; later he leaves home to earn his own living, marries, and eventually must separate finally from immediate values on his deathbed. I do not mean that these events are necessarily actual crises, though they are always *potential* ones; I mean rather to indicate that all growth consists of the anxiety-creating surrender of past values as one transforms them into broader ones. Growth, and with it normal anxiety, consists of the giving up of immediate security for the sake of more extensive goals, death being the final step in this continuum. Hence, Paul Tillich eloquently urged in his book *The Courage to Be* that normal anxiety is synonymous with the "finiteness" of man. Each human being knows he will die, though not when; he anticipates his death through self-awareness. Facing this normal anxiety of finiteness and death may, indeed, be an individual's most effective incentive to make the most of the months or years before death cuts him down.

The transforming of values, and meeting the related anxiety, is one side of creativity. Man is the valuator who, in the very act of valuing, is engaged in molding his world, making himself adequate to his environment and his environment adequate to himself. This interrelation of transforming of values and creativity indicates why creativity has always been considered, from the myth of Prometheus on down, as unavoidably connected with anxiety.

I wish to underline three implications for therapy in this discussion.

First, the goal of therapy is not to free the patient from anxiety. It is, rather, to help free him from neurotic anxiety in order that he may meet normal anxiety constructively. Indeed, *the only way he can achieve the former is to do the latter*. Normal anxiety, we have seen, is an inseparable part of growth and creativity; the self becomes more integrated and stronger as experiences of normal anxiety are successfully confronted. Hence the famous saying of Kierkegaard: "I would say that learning to know anxiety is an adventure which every man has to affront if he would not go to perdition either by not having known anxiety or by sinking under it. He therefore who has learned rightly to be anxious has learned the most important thing."

Second, our discussion implies grave questions about the use of drugs to relieve anxiety. (I except the cases in which anxiety, if not relieved, would itself lead to more serious breakdown, or needs to be relieved to the point where psychotherapy is possible.) The harmful effect of the general use of such drugs is obvious, for to wipe away the anxiety is in principle to wipe away the opportunity for growth, i.e., the possibility of value transformation, of which anxiety is the obverse side. By the same token, neurotic anxiety is a symptom of the fact that some previous crisis has not been met, and to remove the symptom without helping the person get at his underlying conflict is to rob him of his best direction-finder and motivation for self-understanding and new growth.

Third, this chapter implies that there is an inverse relation between the soundness of an individual's value system and his anxiety. That is, the firmer and more flexible your values, the more you will be able to meet anxiety constructively. But the more you are overcome by anxiety, the more your values will diminish in strength. Thus, the patient's arriving at sound values is, in the long run, an integral part of his therapeutic progress. I do not at all mean that the therapist hands over ready-made values to the patient. I do not mean either to relieve the patient of the responsible working out of his own values by permitting him simply to take over the therapist's values. Nor does our argument relieve the therapist of his responsibility to help the patient in the technical process of slow, steady uncovering of the roots of his conflict. Indeed, this has to be done in most cases *before* the patient is able to arrive at his own enduring values.

The criteria for mature values follow from the distinctive characteristics of the human being we discussed earlier: mature values are those which transcend the immediate situation in time and encompass past and future. Mature values transcend also the immediate in-group, and extend outward toward the good of the community, ideally and ultimately embracing humanity as a whole. "I have fallen in love outward," proclaims the young Orestes after his decisive act of autonomy in Robinson Jeffers' play.[6]

The more mature a man's values are, the less it matters to him whether his values are literally satisfied or not. The satisfaction and security lie in the *holding* of the values. To the genuine scientist or religious person or artist, security and confidence arise from his awareness of his devotion to the *search* for truth and beauty rather than the finding of it.

NOTES FOR CHAPTER 5

1. Stewart Wolf, and H. G. Wolff, *Human Gastric Function,* Oxford University Press, New York, 1943.

2. We have already discussed this dialectical capacity of man in Chapter 1, when we related it to the human dilemma and to the work of Portmann.

3. I think that it is very important in experimental work with human beings, in anxiety or other areas, to *define the context* of the particular person being studied; to ask, that is, what symbolic meaning he gives the situation, and what his values are in the experiment at that particular moment. Or if the experimentor is isolating a particular reaction from the self-aware human being, this too should be made evident and defined. For the real meaning of neurophysiological data as well as data of other sorts will be understood only as it is seen in the context of the self-aware person, that is, the person as valuating.

4. Cf. reference to Heisenberg in Chapter 1.

5. I do not, of course, refer here to the fad and cultist interests in Eastern thought, nor to the flight of Western man to Oriental ways of thinking to escape the realities of our own anxiety and alienation.

6. Robinson Jeffers, *The Tower Beyond Tragedy,* New York, 1925.

Part Three

Psychotherapy

Psychotherapy is not only the art and science of assisting people for whom the dilemmas of existence have become especially severe and difficult. It is also an excellent source of data—indeed in many ways our richest source—for understanding these dilemmas and how they may be met. Since the existential approach in psychotherapy has been the one which has most assiduously and directly—if at times with more daring than elegance—dealt with these human dilemmas and insisted they be confronted, we shall deal here particularly with that approach to therapy.

6

The Context of Psychotherapy

MACBETH: *Canst thou not minister to a mind diseas'd,*
Pluck from the memory a rooted sorrow,
Raze out the written troubles of the brain,
And with some sweet oblivious antidote
Cleanse the stuff'd bosom of that perilous stuff
Which weighs upon the heart?
DOCTOR: *Therein the patient*
Must minister to himself. . . .
—SHAKESPEARE, Macbeth

I should like to make clear at the outset the relation of my views to what is called existential psychology and psychiatry. I am trained in psychoanalysis in the neo-Freudian, interpersonal school, but all my life I have been one who believes that the nature of man himself must be understood as a basis for our science and art of psychotherapy. The existential developments in our culture, whether in literature, art, philosophy or science, have precisely as their *raison d'être* the seeking of this understanding of man. Therefore I valued these developments long before I heard about contemporary existential psychiatry in Europe. But I am not an existentialist in the cultist European sense. I think that we in America have to develop approaches that are indigenous to our own experience, and that we must discover what we need in our own historical situations—an attitude in itself which, in my judgment, is the only "existential" one.

The phenomenological and existential development in psychiatry and psychology has been prominent in Europe for several decades.

Whether one likes the terms or not, the issues leading to that development are genuinely important and need to be confronted directly. There are several emphases in this movement that I believe are of special value and which may well be of increasing value in the future development of psychiatry and psychology. Let me begin with three such emphases.

The first is a *new way of seeing the reality of the patient called phenomenology*.[1] The phenomenological method was given its particular contemporary form on the continent of Europe by the work of Edmund Husserl. It is essentially and in simplest terms the endeavor to take the phenomenon as given. The phenomenologists stand against the tendency in Western culture, particularly in the Anglo-Saxon countries, to explain things exclusively by their causes. When in teaching my classes of psychologists and psychiatrists, I cite an example of neurotic or psychotic behavior and ask what it means, the answers which are given by the students almost always have to do not with what the experience means but *why* the patient does it. "He does this *because* . . ." and "The genesis of this is . . ." are the usual phrases. For example, if I ask, "What is shame?" nine out of ten answers will deal with why shame develops, and say nothing whatever about what shame is. We tend to assume that if we have a causal explanation or if we describe how things develop, then we have described the thing itself. This is an error. The phenomenologists hold that we must cut through the tendency in the West to believe we understand things if we only know their causes, and to find out and describe instead what the thing is as a phenomenon—the experience, as it is given to us, in its "givenness." First, that is, we must know what we are talking about. This is not to rule out causation and genetic development, but rather to say that the question of *why* one is what one is does not have meaning until we know *what* one is.

As a therapist, I find that both I and my students get into interminable binds trying to figure out the cause-and-effect pattern of the patient's shame, for example. But if we ask, "What is he trying to say by this blushing? What is the experience in its immediate givenness?" we find ourselves not only freed from the vicious circle but often able to offer a sudden illumination of what the shame is all about. The phenomenological approach not only adds richness and a liveness to the data, but also makes patterns of behavior accessible which were previously a foreign language.

The second emphasis in the existential psychotherapeutic approach is the principle that *all* ways of understanding men, all methods of psychotherapy, are based on some presuppositions, and each approach needs continually to examine these presuppositions. This point comes out clearly in an exchange of correspondence that is now quite famous; I propose to quote parts of it from the little book called *Sigmund Freud—Reminiscences of a Friendship* (Binswanger, 1957).[2] This is an exchange between Ludwig Binswanger, a leading existential psychiatrist, and his close and dear friend, Freud. Binswanger, incidentally, was the only man with whom Freud remained in close friendship even though he differed radically in theory.

Binswanger had been invited by the Vienna Society of Medical Psychology to give an address at the celebration of Freud's eightieth birthday. He delivered a classical paper, only recently translated into English,[3] in which he held that Freud had advanced the understanding of man as a part of nature more than anyone since Aristotle. But he went on to point out that Freud dealt with *homo natura,* that is, natural man, man in what the Germans call the *Umwelt,* the environment, the natural world of drives and instincts. Freud dealt only epiphenomenally with man in the *Mitwelt,* that is, man as fellowman, in interpersonal relationships (in Sullivan's term); nor did Freud deal adequately with the self in relation to itself, namely, the *Eigenwelt.* Hence, Binswanger continued, art, religion, love (in its full sense), creativity, and other human activities in which man transcends the simple natural world environment, are not adequately dealt with in Freud's psychoanalysis.

Because of age and infirmity, Freud did not attend the meeting. ("Celebrations are too much in the American mode!" Freud wrote this friend.) But on reading the address, he wrote a letter to Binswanger in which he stated his appreciation, adding, "Naturally, for all that you have failed to convince me." Then Freud stated

"Probably our differences will be ironed out only after centuries." Binswanger then points out in his book, "As can be seen from the last sentence of Freud, Freud looked upon our differences as something to be surmounted by empirical investigation, not as something bearing upon the transcendental conceptions that underlie all empirical research." [4]

I hope Binswanger's point is clear, despite the fact that the word *transcendental* is a red flag to American psychologists. He means that a concept is prior to the research, and "transcends" it in that your concept already determines what kind of data you will permit yourself to see in your research. The natural science view of man which Freud held, along with its economic model, already would "sieve" and "select" the data of the "empirical research" to fit that presupposition. This is not at all a matter of the research being poor; it is rather a simple characteristic of human observation— you see what your microscope or telescope is focused to take in. Binswanger meant, thus, that the real differences between him and Freud had to do with the assumptions and presuppositions about the nature of man, and how to study him. And he is pointing out that Freud finds it impossible to conceive of the fact that all research is based upon presuppositions.

The critical battles between approaches to psychology and psychoanalysis in our culture in the next decades, I propose, will be on the battleground of the image of man—that is to say, on the conceptions of man which underlie the empirical research. The error Binswanger attacked is no more clearly illustrated than in the assumption so prominent in America that somehow scientific research is the one thing that has no presuppositions! It is as though one believed he can stand outside his own skin and perch on some Archimedean point from which he shall survey all experience; as though we had a godlike perspective that does not itself depend upon the assumptions we make about the nature of man, or the nature of whatever we are studying; or as though we could fondly overlook the fact that our own experience is at every moment molding the instrument by which we study other experience.

Freud was a child of the modern Western age in this respect

and in this error. Every approach in psychotherapy or empirical research unavoidably has its assumptions and presuppositions. Every scientific approach is historically conditioned, just as are religious or artistic approaches of whatever kind.[5] And we can approach objectivity only to the extent that we analyze the presuppositions on which we stand.

The error that comes from not realizing this seems to me to be shown most vividly in the present contradictory form of many psychoanalytic concepts. Take, for example, the concept of ego. In traditional psychoanalysis, this is the organizing principle in the personality, the principle by which some union of the different aspects of personality is achieved in consciousness. But of late years, psychoanalysts in the Freudian tradition have been pointing out that there are many different egos in the same person. They indicate, for example, that there is the "observing portion of the ego," and there is the "repressing portion"; the "reality ego," the "pleasure ego," and so forth.[6] Some of my highly intelligent colleagues in New York now speak of "multiple egos" within the same person. And they are referring to *normal,* not neurotic people. But how can these many *different* egos become a *principle of unity?* Freud, to begin with, described the ego as occupying a most difficult and weak position, buffeted by the Id on one side, Superego on another, and the demands of the world on a third side. This contemporary decking out the poor ego in layer after layer of new clothes does not change the presuppositions inherent in the original concept. These presuppositions were borrowed from Freud's natural scientific, economic model of describing the personality on the basis of "a dynamic conception which reduces mental life to the interaction of reciprocally propelling and repelling forces." Now if the ego comes out of such an assumption, it simply cannot become an adequate organizing principle. *Indeed, no organizing principle is possible except the impersonal play of forces.* The ego is bound, when it is pressed to take over organizing, to become a multiple group of kings, all relatively weak, trying to sit on the same thrones and like as not falling between the thrones.[7]

Is not the picture of multiple egos a contradiction in terms? The very meaning of ego, namely, the unifying principle, has then vanished. Now the error is not in the clinical observations, but rather in the a priori concept itself. It is in this concept that the possibility of unity is destroyed.

All of this demonstrates that we must ask our question on a deeper level, namely, *"At what point is the person himself conscious of the fact that he is these different egos?"* At what point can I be aware that I am the man who has these various tendencies— moods, pleasures, realities, or what not? Now at the point where you can ask the question, "How may I be conscious of the fact that I am the being of whom these different egos are an expression?" you are asking the question on the ontological level, a point we shall return to presently.

I do not think we can have any consistency in our psychoanalytic development or research until we can ask the question on this level, for this is the question that underlies the separate components of the research. The problem in dealing with components of behavior is always, *what assumption do you make by which you select these components to study? And in what form do you propose to unite them?* You must assume some form of relationship between the components, and you must unite them in some way or other. This is the point that requires an investigation of the underlying conceptions which are assumed. Indeed, my point is a highly positive one: for the *principle* by which you select, and the *form* which may hopefully unite your observations, are your creative contribution to the problem. Anyone can do the research, if I may say so, if he is careful, intelligent, and conscientious; but the original contribution lies in seeing a new *form* for the problem. We cannot expect our mathematics and our methodology to assume the burden of our integrity. There is, I am insisting, no escape from the necessity for each one of us to admit and clarify as far as is possible the principles and forms in his own presuppositions.

The third emphasis of the existential psychotherapeutic approach stems directly from the first two and goes by the thorny term "ontology." We have already mentioned it above when we referred to asking the "ontological question." The word "ontology" comes from the Greek *onto-* (being) and *logos* (science) and is the science or study of being. All I have said so far, with respect to phenomenology and the presuppositions on which our research and understanding of psychotherapy are based, pushes us toward this problem. The existential approach holds that we must ask the question of the nature of the man as man, that is to say, the ontological question. I want only to introduce the term here and will return to it later.

LET US NOW move into a more specific application of these principles. And let us begin with the question, What is our basic unit of study in psychotherapy? It is a very curious situation, when you come to think of it, that somebody comes to a therapist's office and sits there in a chair within a strange world of four walls with some expectation that he may be helped. How would one describe the unit of study in that situation? Does one describe it as a patient with a problem—a problem of flunking out of college, inability to love or marry, or what not? That would be the oldtime way of defining a patient as a problem—the "gallbladder on the seventh floor," as my medical patients say is still the vernacular in some hospitals—and deprecates both the patient and the situation. Shall we say, rather, that here is a patient who is hysterical or compulsive, psychotic or neurotic, with such and such symptoms? This is the usual form of identification in our day, but I submit that it is also partial and therefore inadequate. It implies that we do not see him as a person but as a set of diagnostic categories about him which can too readily become the confining spectacles through which our perceptions are sieved.

Or shall we say, here is a person who has a problem and comes to the therapist because he wants to get well? This gets closer to the real situation. But it is, unfortunately, precisely what we don't know; we cannot be sure that this person wants to get well. We can indeed be sure getting well is precisely what he is ambivalent about; he comes needing to remain ill until other aspects in his existence are changed. He comes in conflict and his motives are in all probability very much confused.

So what is our unit of study? I suggest we can say to start with:

we have two persons in a given space, in a given world. By "world" here I mean, as in the classical sense of the word, a structure of meaningful relationships. These two people, patient and therapist, have different motives for being here. We do not know the motives of the patient; he got here, however, and therefore some meaningful act is involved.

It is at this point that I, as therapist, must make some ontological assumptions, whether I admit it or not. (And I am arguing that it is much healthier for all concerned if the therapist can admit and frankly clarify to himself such assumptions.) My patient sits there in the chair. I know practically nothing about him. But I can assume that *he, like all living organisms, seeks to preserve some center, and I assume he is here in the chair in my office in the process of doing that.* The first ontological characteristic, thus, is that all human beings are potentially centered in themselves, no matter how much that centeredness is distorted in conflict.[8] I assume in the same breath that this man (like all organisms) has the character of self-affirmation, that is, the need to preserve his centeredness. These I propose as ontological characteristics of man as man. Here Paul Tillich's (1952) concept of the *courage to be* is of fundamental importance. The tree's centeredness—which is marvelously developed in balance and unity, as anyone looking at a well-grown tree can tell—is given automatically. But the human being's centeredness depends upon his courage to affirm it—albeit that courage often affirms it in highly neurotic ways. Tillich holds that if we do not have courage, we lose our being. Man is the particular creature in nature whose being depends upon his courage; and if he is not able, because of the degree of pathology or terribly adverse external circumstances to affirm his being, he gradually loses it.

Another thing to be noticed about this patient who has come to my office is that immediately there is a relationship. Even in anticipation when I or the patient thinks of the meeting, there is a relationship—which indicates that I assume relationship before I can observe whether he looks at me or away or listens too eagerly or not at all. The patient, like all beings *has the need and possibility of going out from his centeredness* to participate in other beings. He is now struggling with the possibility of participating with the therapist. This going out always involves risk.

Here and in the next chapter I am presenting sickness and health, and specifically neurosis, with a quite different meaning from any generally given them in our society. From the ontological approach that I have suggested, we see *that sickness is precisely the method that the individual uses to preserve his being.* We cannot assume in the usual oversimplified way that the patient automatically wants to get well; we must assume, rather, that he cannot permit himself to give up his neurosis, to get well, until other conditions in his existence and his relation to his world are changed. Neurosis is an adjustment activity which has within it the creative potential of the individual that must in one way or another be shifted to the constructive goals in his process of overcoming his problems. The neurotic is the "artiste manqué," said Otto Rank, and the neurosis has within it the potentialities which we hope will be called forth and redirected in psychotherapy.

The next thing we observe[9] about this patient who now sits in front of the therapist, is that he is participating with the therapist on a level of *awareness* which I propose as the fourth ontological characteristic. I use awareness now as a characteristic that is shared by forms of life other than human. A cat will leap away if you raise a stick; he is certainly aware of the physical threat to his centeredness. The biologist von Uexküll has described how different organisms have different blueprints; he calls them "action plans" and "perception plans" with respect to their worlds. The trees and plants are relatively tied to their particular worlds; animals possess a greater degree of freedom with respect to the world; and human beings have the greatest degree of freedom of all. This range increases with the range of awareness, that is, the range of possibilities in relating to the world.

But the principle of awareness itself is not enough. So we arrive at the distinctive form of awareness in human beings, namely *self-consciousness.* I have long believed that the tendency to substitute the term "awareness" for "consciousness" in our psychological work is ill-advised. True, awareness more easily fits the conventional scientific framework; it is more amenable to being broken into components, to being studied and experimented with in discrete situations and with mechanistic models in animals and man. Consciousness, on the other hand, is much harder to deal with in research, for it is characterized by the fact that if we break it up into components, we lose what we are studying. The word, "awareness," comes from the root Anglo-Saxon term, *gewaer,* which in turn comes from *waer,* which refers in this whole family of terms to knowledge of external threats—that is, knowledge of danger, of enemies, knowledge requiring defensive strategies. The cognates of this word, "aware" are the terms "wary" and "beware." Awareness is the correct category for Howard Liddell to use, as he does, in his studies of so-called animal neurosis. He calls awareness their *vigilance.* He describes the seal, for example, in its natural habitat, lifting its head every ten seconds to survey the horizon to make sure that no Eskimo with bow and arrow is sneaking up. Liddell identifies this vigilance as the primitive, simple counterpart in animals of what in human beings becomes anxiety.

Consciousness, on the other hand, from the Latin verb *conscire,* refers to knowledge which is felt *inwardly,* that is, to *knowing with,* not only with others but with oneself in the sense of consciousness of the fact that I am the being who has a world. I can be *aware* of this desk on which I write simply by touching it. But *consciousness* refers rather to the fact that *I can be aware that I am the being who has this desk.* Consciousness is related to my conception of myself as the being who uses the desk as he struggles with these ideas which he endeavors to make clear in writing. Consciousness is a term that must not be lost. It refers to the central ontological characteristic that constitutes the self in its existence as a self, namely, the experience that I can be aware that I am the being who has a world. We are using the term in the sense of Kurt Goldstein's (1939) description of the capacity of the human being to transcend the immediate situation, to use abstractions and universals, to communicate in language and symbols, and on the basis of these capacities, to survey and actualize in one form or another the greater range of possibilities (greater compared to animal and inanimate nature) in relating to oneself, one's fellows, and one's world. In this sense, human freedom has its ontological basis and must be assumed in all psychotherapy.

I propose that unconscious experience can be understood only on the basis of our concept of consciousness. We must posit that the patient comes as a potential unity, no matter how clearly we can see that various neurotic symptoms have been blocked off and thereby have a compulsive effect upon him. I am not saying this unity is necessarily a good one—as I have indicated in talking of the "unity of adjustment," it may be a very limiting one. But the neurotic's very symptoms, disruptive and disjunctive as they appear to us on the outside, are expressions of his endeavor to preserve his unity. To preserve this unity he has to block off, refuse to actualize, some potentialities for knowledge and action.

Now "unconsciousness" consists of the experiences that the person cannot permit himself to actualize. The questions in understanding unconscious phenomena are, "How does this individual reject or accept his possibilities for being conscious of himself and his world?" "How is it possible that he should shut out something which on another level he knows, and even *knows that he knows?*" The thing that continually surprises patients in psychoanalysis, and even sometimes surprises the analyst, is that when a buried memory or experience which has been subjected to radical repression erupts into consciousness, the patient will often report that he has the sudden strange experience of having known it all the time. On the level of awareness, this makes no sense at all: he has not been able to be aware of it. But he *has* on another level known it all the time; it has been present in the fact that he has had to repress it. The problem that we should set ourselves, then, is not solely or even chiefly the mechanical one of what particular trauma blocked off the experience. Rather, it is the question of what is going on in this person that he cannot let himself fully experience "I am I; I am this being with all the potentialities and possibilities that constitute this being, this I."

Note that I do not say that the original trauma which hypothetically led to the repression should be ignored. I say that it in itself does not account for the *persistence* of the repression, nor is it the main reason he still represses the experience.

I WANT NOW to explore the problem of the emergence and meaning of consciousness by referring to the Oedipus myth and complex. The Oedipus situation is taken as basic in Freud's work, as we all know, and is present in practically all other schools of therapy in some form or other. In Freud's formulation, it refers to the sexual love attraction between a child and the parent of the opposite sex. The child thereby experiences guilt and fear of the parent of whom he is the rival, and particularly in the case of boys, fear of castration. Fromm refers to the Oedipus conflict of the growing child as the struggle with the authority of the parents. Adler sees it as a power struggle.

Now Freud assumed in his Oedipal description a tragic picture of human experience. The infant was cannibalistic, driven by primitive instinctual demands; Freud's view of the infant was similar to St. Augustine's, who said, "The innocence of the child consists of weakness of limb." Freud's tragic view, that in the Oedipal situation there is a genuine conflict between beings who on some level are engaged in destroying each other, is to my mind closer to the truth of the Oedipal situation than the general optimistic and oversimplified view in America. Our view is that of Rousseau's—that the infant is not a cannibal but either an angel, if he is our own, or potentially an angel if he is the child of somebody we are counseling. He is potentially an angel if only those mothers and other cultural representatives would feed him with more care, meet his needs and train him correctly. Thus in the Oedipus conflict, as taken over in our thought in this country, the tragic aspect, by and large, is omitted. But the tragic quality is precisely the reason that Freud hit upon the Oedipal myth to begin with. I think it is a considerable loss that the tragic emphases that are present in Freud are the first things thrown overboard when psychoanalysis crosses the Atlantic Ocean.

I want to propose a third approach. This is the approach of

understanding the Oedipal situation as the tragic conflict within the person, and in his relations to his world and other human beings involved, in the emergence and development of consciousness of himself. If you look back at the Oedipus drama in Sophocles or in other forms given to us in its long cultural history, you will discover that it is not a play about sexual conflicts or conflicts over killing the father. These are all long done and past. In Sophocles' drama Oedipus has married his mother; he is a good king, and is happy and comfortable in Thebes.

The only question in the drama is, shall Oedipus recognize what he has done? The tragic issue is the issue of seeing the reality and the truth about oneself. The drama, we recall, opens with the curse on Thebes. In order to have that curse lifted, Oedipus, the present king of Thebes, must find out who killed Laius, the preceding king. Oedipus calls Tiresias, the blind seer. In the drama, Tiresias is associated with the role of a psychoanalyst; his not seeing externally is symbolically related to the capacity for greater sensitivity within. Hence the historical symbol of "the blind prophet." Blind men, not distracted by the external things they do not see, are in this symbolic form thought to develop a greater sensitivity to truth in a psychological and spiritual sense. I trust this can carry over and apply to psychologists and psychiatrists without our having necessarily to be physically blind.

Oedipus asks Tiresias who is guilty. Tiresias responds,

> I will not bring remorse upon myself
> And upon you. Why do you search these matters?

Oedipus insists that regardless of consequences, he must know who killed Laius. Then step by step through the drama we see an amazing portrayal of the struggle—ultimately a tragic struggle—of a man, Oedipus, struggling to discover the truth about himself. First he finds out the truth about his objective situation, the death of his father, and then discovers the truth turned inward, becoming truth about himself. He senses soon that there is a mystery that surrounds his own birth, and that Jocasta, his mother, whom he has married without knowing the relationship, is somehow associated with the mystery of his birth. (It will be recalled that he had been taken out by Laius and abandoned on the hillside because of the oracle's prediction that he, Oedipus, would kill his father.)

In the course of the dramatic "analysis," Jocasta suddenly becomes aware that Oedipus is her son. Then she realizes also the terrible knowledge that confronts him and tries to dissuade him. She cries,

> . . . But why should men be fearful,
> O'er whom Fortune is mistress, and foreknowledge
> Of nothing sure? Best take life easily,
> As a man may. For that maternal wedding,
> Have no fear; for many men ere now
> Have dreamed as much; but he who by such dreams
> Sets nothing, has the easiest time of it.

Let me interject here that all too often our psychoanalytic and our psychiatric and our psychological relationships with patients are of the nature of Jocasta's speech. What she really is saying is, "Be adjusted. Do not take dreams as reality. Many people 'ere now have dreamed as much,' but never let such things bother you."

Oedipus, however, will not stop at this point; his dreams are his being. He says in effect, "I must have the courage to face the truth whatever it is."

And then Jocasta cries out,

> Don't seek it! I am sick, and that's enough . . .
> Wretch, what thou art O mightst thou never know!

But Oedipus returns,

> I will not hearken—not to know the whole,
> Break out what will, I shall not hesitate . . .

He concludes, "I must know who I am and where I am from." Toward the end of the play, he searches out the old shepherd who had found him as a baby up on the hillside and kept him alive. The shepherd, being called in answer to Oedipus' question, moans, "O, I am at the horror, now, to speak!" And Oedipus answers, "And I to hear. But I must hear—no less."

Then he does learn the tragic truth, that he is the one who killed his father and married his mother. Thereupon, *he plucks out his eyes, the organ of seeing and recognition.* Finally, he exiles himself. I think this theme of exile is very important: he was exiled as a baby—that is where the tragedy started. Now, he exiles *himself*. This is significant also because of contemporary man's fear of ostracism. The tragedy of exile, the tragedy of man alienated from his fellowmen, is very close to the central psychological problems of contemporary men in the middle of the twentieth century.

The drama is the tragedy of seeing the reality about oneself, confronting what one is and what one's origin is, the tragedy of a man knowing and facing in conscious self-knowledge his own destiny. The verbs all the way through, we observe, are *knowing, hearing, discovering, seeing*.

Let me illustrate this by citing a dream of a patient of mine. The dream is one of a long series, and therefore is presented in truncated, although I hope clear, form. It is a dream of an intelligent, sensitive woman of thirty who was greatly blocked in her professional activity and in her sexual role (she had been married and divorced and had a good deal of sexual experience, but never had experienced orgasm). Her parents were well-to-do intellectuals who, from her birth until she was three, had abandoned the girl most of the time and gone to Europe. She suffered very strong feelings of isolation, anxiety, and hostility, and early in life she had learned to play roles in order to be accepted. She described a very obvious and pronounced Oedipal relation to her father, who, now dead, had been a gifted and weak man; and she also had the customary strong rivalry with her mother.

Like a drama, the dream occurred in three scenes which were progressive. In the first scene she met her former husband, who had come back from Europe married, in a dentist's office. Two of his front teeth were missing. He introduced her to his new wife and two children. She realized that she could not have been that kind of wife to him, and she accepted and affirmed the fact that he was happily married now. In the second scene of the dream she was standing vis à vis some feminine person, and she was feeling and playing a masculine role; then she was vis à vis some masculine person and playing the feminine role. She thought to herself in the dream, "I have always tried to be these different things." The third scene in the dream she related in these words: "I was with another person, a man with whom I could be myself; there were no roles anymore. I could be my feminine self. It was a tremendous experience. Then I found myself looking down into a stream, and I experienced a great anxiety; I had the feeling I would have to jump into the river and commit suicide."

The associations to the dream were in her mind fairly obvious. The first part implied that she now could accept her husband's marriage; the two missing front teeth referred, she said, to the fact that she had castrated him, which she had. Fortunately, the two missing teeth could be fixed. (I think the dentist's office—an unflattering comparison, incidentally, that comes up not infrequently with patients—is the office of the psychoanalyst to whom her husband goes.) In the second part of the dream she saw herself trying on these roles for size as though saying to me, "This is what I have been doing all my life." The third scene relates the tremendously important experience of being herself, throwing off the roles with the great relief involved. All of this she saw in the dream. But what she could not understand was the terrible anxiety, the feeling that she would have to jump into a river and commit suicide. As we too try to understand the dream, we need to keep in mind that it was an exceedingly constructive dream, a radical landmark in her psychotherapy. It actually foreshadowed a breakthrough in several ways, for example, in her capacity to have orgasm.

So why all the anxiety? One could say she was giving up her defenses, giving up the roles by which she had been able to survive since her early childhood, roles that had been absolutely essential to her. One could also say she was cutting through rationalizations and illusions about herself, for example, in the admission that she had castrated her husband. But something else was taking place on a more basic level in this dream. It was a tragic recognition of fate itself—I borrow the word fate from Freud, and I use it now in the sense of the Oedipus drama. When one is able to be aware in his self-consciousness that he is the person who is the conscious responsible being, there comes pronounced anxiety, a potentially tragic anxiety. I think it is fair to say that a good many, if not most, therapists would tend at this point to reassure the patient. The patient's anxiety is obviously over being herself, and the tendency would be to say, "Yes, you have had to cut out all of these roles and these methods that you have used to gain security; but now you can be yourself and you do not need to be anxious about it."

I propose, on the contrary, that she does need to be anxious about it; and that this is precisely the constructive aspect of the mature, tragic anxiety that is shown in the drama of Oedipus. The symbol of suicide, the capacity to confront death, is placed in a central position in the existential approach in psychology and psychiatry. These things are not negations, though they are a tragic aspect of life. The capacity to confront death is a prerequisite to growth, a prerequisite to self-consciousness. I take the orgasm here as a psychophysical symbol. It is the experience of the capacity to abandon oneself, to give up present security in favor of wider experience. It is not by accident that the orgasm often appears symbolically as a partial death and rebirth; and it should not surprise us that this capacity to "give oneself up," to "risk oneself," should have had as one of its manifestations her being able after the dream to experience a sexual orgasm.

If one looks further into this dream, one will see a fascinating myth involved. Though it is fairly obvious that the man in the third scene of the dream is myself (the Hudson River flows outside my office window in New York), there is something much more profound occurring than what can be described in the context simply of the relationship with me. The second myth is the myth of going under water, being drowned and born again, a myth that is passed down in different religions and different cultures—namely, baptism. To be drowned in order to be born again—this is the myth of the positive integrative aspect of experiencing truth. This integrative aspect is present also in the Oedipus myth: Sophocles fortunately wrote a subsequent play, *Oedipus at Colonus,* in which the old king meditates about all of the tragic events that have happened to him in his distraught life. In doing this, Oedipus experiences the reconciliation with himself, the new unity that occurs after the tragic experience of consciousness.

Some readers will not be happy with that phrase "the tragic experience of consciousness," and would prefer to tone down the phrase. I choose to use the strong words even though they have connotations that are misleading. If we want to inquire psychologically what this tragic aspect of consciousness means, it is not difficult to describe it. First, it certainly involves admitting what we have done: "If I am Oedipus, I have killed my father," that is, admitting our destructive attitudes and behavior toward people we may genuinely love. Secondly, it means admitting our present motives of hatred and destructiveness. Thirdly, it means cutting through our rationalizations about our own nobility. At this point, we arrive at an existential level, for to cut through these rationalizations implies not only taking responsibility for "what I did yesterday" but responsibility for "what I shall do and feel and think tomorrow." This attitude implies another corollary, namely, aloneness. At the point where I am aware that I am this being, this one who is acting, who killed his father or castrated her husband, I am at a point where nobody else can stand. No matter what the extenuating circumstances, this is *my* hatred and *my* destructiveness; and at this point a man relates to himself in a state of aloneness. I am the only one who can take that responsibility.

This tragic consciousness also implies—and this is the most difficult point of all—that a person recognizes the fact that he never can love completely the people to whom he is devoted, and there will always remain some elements of destructiveness. The emphases that Freud made here are of great importance. By the same token, we can never know absolutely whether a decision we now make is really the right decision; nevertheless, we must make the decision anyway. This risk inheres in self-consciousness. I think it involves the giving up of childhood omnipotence; we are no longer God, to put it symbolically. But we must act as though we were; we must act as though our decisions were right. This is the reaching out into the future that makes all of life a risk and makes all experience precarious.

Down this line I think we shall find the most profound meaning of consciousness. I have pointed it out only briefly, though we could discuss it endlessly. This is why there is such a close relationship between development of consciousness and psychosis. When people, in therapy, go through these emergent levels of consciousness, they often have the fear of becoming psychotic. I propose these deeper reaches of the problem of consciousness for further study.

I SHOULD LIKE to close with some practical comments about the goals of therapy. What I have said implies that anxiety and guilt are never wholly negative phenomena. It implies that some of our general assumptions about mental health—for example, that mental health consists of freedom from anxiety—are inaccurate. Our goals with respect to anxiety and guilt should be not to wipe them out (as though we could even if we wanted to!) but to help people, our patients and ourselves, to confront anxiety and guilt constructively. It is sometimes said that in psychoanalysis at certain points one has to inject anxiety into the patient, otherwise he basks forever in the warmth of the relationship. But I believe that we only have to inject anxiety if we have watered it down to begin with. I think a great deal of our error lies in a tendency to reassure anxiety, to dilute it, and to do the same with guilt feeling. I believe, rather, that the function of therapy is to give people a context in which they are able to confront and experience anxiety and guilt constructively—a context which is a human world, as well as a real world, of a person's own existence in relation to the therapist.

It may clarify matters if I differentiate between neurotic and normal anxiety. Neurotic anxiety is anxiety which is inappropriate to the threat of a situation. It involves repression into unconsciousness. It is expressed in symptom formation. It has destructive rather than constructive effects upon the organism. I think the same criteria could be given for guilt feelings, though the area of guilt feeling is more controversial. "Normal" anxiety would now be accepted by most psychologists and psychiatrists much as I have described it; but between normal and neurotic guilt feeling there is still a battle line. In general, our colleagues do not like the concept of normal guilt feeling.

Normal guilt, in contrast to neurotic guilt, is guilt that is appropriate to the situation. The woman whose dream I cited did castrate her husband and did hurt him (as well as he her, of course). In the dream she has accepted normal guilt. Secondly, there was no repression into unconsciousness. This was a wholesome change—her guilt toward her husband for a long time had been simply repressed under the idea that, "Well, he deserves it, look what he does to me." Thirdly, conscious or normal guilt does not involve symptom formation. It does not involve, for example, symptoms of self-righteousness. Repressed guilt shows itself very often in insistence that one is right, in lack of humility, lack of capacity to be open to the other person, etc. Normal guilt is associated with admitting that one can know only partially, and involves admitting that what one says always does partial violence to the truth. We can only partially understand each other; this is normal guilt. It helps us to do the best we can in presenting our thoughts to each other, and it also gives us a humility as we communicate that makes us more sensitive and more open to each other. Fourthly, normal guilt has a constructive effect.

To clarify our discussion of this topic, which is at best bound to be confused, I need to say that my position with respect to guilt is very different from that of Hobart Mowrer. Mowrer did make a real contribution in his early point that modern people are made "ill" not only by repressing the "Id" in the Freudian sense, but also by repression of the "Super-Ego." The fact that people in our culture repress their consciences is indeed true and important. But Mowrer's therapy then becomes a bringing of the super-ego back into the patient's life. This constitutes a new authoritarianism. For the therapist to reinforce the mores of society as a "solving" of the problem of guilt feeling is to make the patient less autonomous and responsible in the long run with respect to himself and the conflicts which underlie his guilt feeling. After the development of self-consciousness in the growing individual, the conflicts are never the simple issue of the individual versus society, but have taken on symbolic meaning which is of the greatest importance. (Psychopaths are the one clinical entity which constitutes an exception to this point.) If the therapist's chief approach is the strengthening of social mores, I believe he sets the stage for the generation of later neurotic guilt in the patient.[10]

Let us also clarify the relation between shame and guilt. Shame has to guilt somewhat the same relation as fear has to anxiety. If fear is the specific objectified form of reaction to a threat, it can be dealt with as a unit in itself and can be experimented upon; it can be described on the level of awareness, can be objectified. Fear is removed when the specific external cause is removed. But anxiety is the general, the underlying common denominator of the person's capacity to experience threat, to experience his precarious situation. Anxiety, therefore, must be the generic term and fear can be only understood as an objectified form of anxiety. Is the situation not parallel to shame and guilt? Shame can be understood in relation to a specific incident, say, if I were the compulsively correct type and I mispronounced a word, I might blush. But we cannot understand that blush of mine unless we are able to relate it to some underlying stratum in my personality, which then will be the problem of guilt, neurotic guilt, probably, in such a case. In this formulation, guilt is the generic term and shame the specific form of guilt, objectivated and attached to a special social incident.

I think that normal guilt must be dealt with existentially, which means that all aspects of the experience must be considered. Normal guilt has as one aspect my relation with my fellowmen. It is the state when I do not live in openness with them, an area in which Martin Buber had contributed significantly. That is, normal guilt hinges conceptually on whether or not one is a *fellow* man, open, humble, loving—if one may use the term in that sense. There is another aspect of normal guilt which inheres in our relationship to ourselves: the extent to which we betray or live out our potentialities, are faithful to needs, powers, sensitivities in ourselves. There is the possibility of normal guilt in all aspects of experience. If I may put the problem in its ultimate formulation, I would express my view as follows: When we are in the process of confronting an issue of whether we shall betray something significant to our being or live it out, realize it, we are in the state of anxiety; when we are aware that we *have* betrayed something significant for our being, we are in the state of guilt. *Neurotic* guilt—as is the case with neurotic anxiety—is simply the end result of unconfronted, repressed *normal* guilt. One can always be specific about the neurotic aspects of these problems, because the neurosis is, by nature and by definition, a truncating of experience; but one cannot be as specific about the positive aspects. All one can say is that a person must be open or free to do whatever is involved, and the guilt must be lived out existentially.

LET ME, FINALLY, say a word about the encounter in the therapeutic relationship. To be able to sit in a real relationship with another human being who is going through profound anxiety or guilt or the experience of imminent tragedy taxes the best of the humanity in all of us. This is why I emphasize the importance of the "encounter" and use that word rather than "relationship." I think the term relationship psychologizes it too much. Encounter is what really happens; it is something much more than a relationship. In this encounter I have to be able, to some extent, to experience what the patient is experiencing. My job as a therapist is to be open to his world. He brings his world with him and therein we live for fifty minutes. Learning to do so may be highly taxing; to experience somebody else's anxiety can be extremely painful. It is painful enough to experience one's own, when one has no choice but to bear one's own world. Practically speaking, this is why therapy for oneself is so important; my own psychoanalysis certainly helped me in being able to accept the anxiety and guilt in patients, not to try to push aside the pain or cover over the tragic possibilities. In addition, the therapeutic encounter requires that we ourselves be human beings in the broadest sense of the word. This brings us to a point where we can no longer talk about it merely psychologically, in any kind of detached way, but must "throw" ourselves into the therapeutic encounter. In this it helps to realize that we also have gone through similar experiences, and though perhaps not involved in them now, we know what they mean. This is part of the grandeur and the misery of man, and this is why reading Sophocles and the other ancient tragedians, I think, is a great help for us as psycho-therapists.

Our chief concern in therapy is with the potentiality of the human being. The goal of therapy is to help the patient actualize his poten-tialities. The joy of the process of actualizing becomes more impor-tant than the pleasure of discharged energy—though that itself, in its own context, obviously has pleasurable aspects too. The goal of therapy is not the absence of anxiety, but rather the changing of neurotic anxiety into normal anxiety, and the development of the capacity to live with and use normal anxiety. The patient after therapy may well bear more anxiety than he had before, but it will be conscious anxiety and he will be able to use it constructively. Nor is the goal the absence of guilt feeling, but rather the transformation of neurotic guilt into normal guilt, together with the development of the capacity to use this normal guilt creatively.

I have proposed here a number of ideas which I realize are left hanging in the air. I have no guilt, however, about the fact that I have left them hanging there. This is what I meant to do. I hope that these ideas, rather than presenting concise answers, will act, like leavening in the loaf, to open up existential psychological expe-riences for others.

NOTES FOR CHAPTER 6

1. I have hesitated about whether to use that term "new," since phenomenology is present in William James (see Chapter 9) and in the work of some contemporary psychologists like Robert McLeod, Gordon Allport, and others. But it has by no means been utilized for the importance and value that it can have in psychology and psy-chotherapy. Gordon Allport (1955) makes the distinction between the Leibnizian tradition and the Lockean. In the countries in which the former is dominant, phenomenology has been the chief method; in the countries where the latter has held sway, such as England and the United States, the dominant methods are behavioristic and operational.

2. Ludwig Binswanger, *Sigmund Freud: Reminiscences of a Friendship,* New York, 1957.

3. Ludwig Binswanger, *Being-in-the-World,* translated with an introduction by Jacob Needleman, Basic Books, New York, 1963.

4. Binswanger, *Sigmund Freud,* p. 99.

5. The implications of this point are probably overlooked in psychology most of all; cf. Chapter 14.

6. Karl Menninger, *Theory of Psychoanalytic Technique,* New York, 1958.

7. This is why I have pointed out elsewhere the inadequacy of the concept of ego for the understanding of human will and decision. Cf. my *Love and Will,* Norton, New York (to be published). Freud himself, we should add, took a different approach in his practical therapy and his own personal life, in both of which he acted on the faith that the human being does have some unity and personal freedom to will. He seems always to have lived and thought within the dilemma between his mechanistic model of the mind, based on determinism, and his existential experience of life, in which we see an individual of remarkably strong will.

8. The reader will note that I make my assumption of centeredness of the organism at the very beginning—rather than at some future "development of the ego stage." The fact that neurosis and psychosis —the breakdown of centeredness—are *sickness* already presupposes the assumption of centeredness.

9. I find myself using the terms "notice" and "observe" when referring to ontological principles about the person while he is actually there. These are principles I *assume* about the human organism qua organism and *observe* specifically in individuals I work with.

10. For a discussion of the authoritarian aspects of Mowrer's therapy, see the whole issue of *Pastoral Psychology* of Oct. 1965, Vol. 16, No. 157. Especially see the article in that issue, "Psychoanalysts, Mowrer and the Existentialists," by Donald F. Krill.

7

A Phenomenological Approach to Psychotherapy

> It is dangerous to show man too often that he is equal
> to beasts, without showing him his greatness. It is also
> dangerous to show him too frequently his greatness
> without his baseness. It is yet more dangerous to leave
> him ignorant of both. But, it is very desirable to show
> him the two together.
>
> BLAISE PASCAL, Pensées

I do not believe there is a special school of therapy to be put in a category of "existential." As I use the term, "existential" refers to an attitude toward human beings and a set of presuppositions about these human beings. Therefore I shall be talking in this chapter about intensive psychotherapy, whether it be of the Freudian, Jungian, Sullivanian, or any other school.

We must admit at the outset that we have not yet built a complete bridge between phenomenology and psychotherapy. There exist beginnings of this bridge; there is the exceedingly important work of Straus and other phenomenological psychiatrists like Minkowski and Binswanger, whose work I believe will be increasingly more important for psychotherapy in the future. And there are psychologists like Buytendijk and phenomenological philosophers who have made very important contributions to psychology like Merleau-Ponty. But as Binswanger himself has been the first to say, the connection between phenomenology and psychotherapy is at present only indirect. Several steps are required between pure phenomenol-

ogy on one hand and psychology and psychiatry on the other hand;
this is given by our existential problem rather than by our lack of
ability to formulate. I certainly do not deny the many interrelation-
ships between phenomenology and different kinds of therapy. But
I believe our present overall task is one of building. When they
build a bridge over the East River in New York, part of the bridge
reaches out from Brooklyn and part from Manhattan; we are in
process of such a construction, with phenomenology on one side and
psychology on the other reaching out toward a meeting. What I want
to do in this chapter is to explore some of the problems in this construction, which means problems in the relationship between psychotherapy and phenomenology.

Jean-Paul Sartre writes, by the same token, that we are not yet
ready to formulate an existential psychoanalysis, arriving at this
conclusion, somewhat ironically, in the chapter entitled, "Existential
Psychoanalysis," in his book, *Being and Nothingness*. I think he is
correct, with respect to both an existential psychoanalysis and even
a phenomenological one. It is significant, incidentally, that Sartre
in his book takes seriously Freud and psychoanalysis and the problems that lie therein—an attitude which we can well commend to
other philosophers.

The initial consideration in understanding the relationship between phenomenology and psychotherapy is that we confront directly
the work of Sigmund Freud. If we try to bypass Freud we shall be
guilty of a kind of suppression. For what Freud thought, wrote,
and performed in therapy, whether one agrees fully with it or not,
permeates our whole culture, our literature and art and almost every
other aspect of Western man's self-interpretation. Freud obviously
had more influence on psychology and psychiatry than any other
man in the twentieth century. Unless we confront him directly, consciously and unflinchingly, our discussions of therapy will always
hang in a vacuum.

We cannot, furthermore, dismiss Freud simply by stating our dis-
agreements with him. One summer twenty-five years ago I was on
an island in Maine finishing a thesis on psychotherapy. A friend
that I made there, a young Catholic priest with whom I used to go

swimming and fishing, happened one day to be up in my room and saw on my shelves a number of books by Freud. He immediately explained to me in twelve succinct sentences why Freud was wrong. Since this was before psychotherapy was read either in Protestant or Catholic theological seminaries, I wondered if he knew anything about the master from Vienna. So I asked if he had read any books by Freud. "Oh, yes," he answered, "everybody in our seminary is required to read one book." I thought this very enlightened, so I inquired the name of the book. The title, he said, was *Freud Refuted*.

This incident always comes back to my mind when I read the writings especially of the deviant schools: I read a great deal about Freud refuted, but what I fail to find is that Freud himself is directly and seriously confronted.

I believe the issue with Freud must be joined on two fronts. We need first to appreciate and ask the meaning of the vast changes, amounting in many ways to sheer revolution, that Freud's impact has had upon Western man's image of himself. And secondly, we need to face the fact that the image of man he consciously sought and worked toward—an image amazingly contradictory at many points to his mythology—is inadequate and must be superseded by an understanding of the nature of man that is adequate to man as the *human* being.[1] I propose that a task that needs to be done is a phenomenological analysis of Freud and the meaning of his impact upon Western culture. Here I can only offer some remarks on how I see the underlying meaning of this impact on our image of man.

First, *Freud tremendously enlarged the realm of human consciousness*. The meaning of his elaboration and elucidation of what he called "the unconscious" (or what I prefer to call "unconscious potentialities of experience") was a radical breaking of Victorian rationalism and voluntarism. I shall deal later with the problem of the "unconscious." Here I want only to emphasize that he uncovered the vast areas in which human behavior and motives are influenced, molded, pushed—and in neurotic cases determined— by forces which are much vaster and more profound and meaningful than those encompassed in Victorian rationalism. His contribution was to enlarge the sphere of human personality to include the depths, i.e., the irrational, the so-called repressed, unacceptable urges, the instinctual forces, bodily drives, anxiety, fears, forgotten aspects of experience, *ad infinitum*.

His lucidation of "wish" and "drive" and his unmasking of the self-deceit of Victorian will power also destroyed moralism in the oversimplified sense in which most of us absorbed it as children. I recall that I was taught as a child in the Middle West that I could completely decide my destiny by any resolution I might make on New Year's Day or in church on any Sunday when the whim might strike me. This amazing piece of arrogance really amounted to my playing God. I have learned since then that God moves in much more mysterious ways—to put it religiously—and that the destiny of myself and other human beings—to put it psychologically— springs from deeper levels in the human heart and psyche than we were led to believe in our liberalized and overenlightened West. This Victorian belief in will power was really the dedication to the manipulation of nature, to the rule of nature with an iron hand (as in industrialism and capitalism) and of one's own body with the same iron hand, and to the manipulation of one's self in a similar way (which is evident not only in the ethics of Protestantism but also in other religious systems of our day, and is particularly present in the nonreligious ethics on Madison Avenue which are not softened by a sense of sin or humanized by a principle of mercy).

Now this manipulation of one's self on the basis of such a concept of moralistic will power needed to be undermined. I am convinced that it was one of Freud's great contributions that by elucidating the infinite number of wishes, drives, and other motivations of which we at any given moment may not be conscious, he made this kind of will power and moralism impossible. Since Freud's time, the moral problem has not been lost but placed on a deeper level; and the problems of guilt and responsibility have to be confronted on this more profound level. Rightly understood, these earthquakes that Freud produced in Western culture, earthquakes that shook the self-picture of modern Western man to its very base, imply a humility that can be very liberating.

I shall later indicate how I believe the inadequacies of Freud lent strength to an undermining of modern man's sense of individual responsibility. But here let me say that there are curious implications in Freud's psychological determinism that we generally overlook, implications which point in the direction of psychological freedom. I notice with my patients the strange fact that their reaction to an interpretation by me often does not center so much on whether the interpretation is true or not as on the liberating implications in *my act* of making an interpretation. The patient seems to be hearing, in my interpretation, the words, "Your problem has deeper inner roots than you realized; you can stand outside it and deal with it." This reminds us of Spinoza's statement, "Freedom is the recognition of determinism."

From these brief indications of how I believe a phenomenological approach to Freud could and should be undertaken, let us move on to explore the relationship between phenomenology and psychotherapy.

WE PSYCHOTHERAPISTS look to phenomenology to give us a road to an understanding of the fundamental nature of man. What we need are norms concerning man which have some degree of universality. Whenever we confront a patient, we presuppose some answer to the question, "What constitutes this being as a *human* being?" We cannot get this understanding of the nature of man from our study of illness, for the various categories of illness themselves can be understood only as distortions in the patient's realization of his human nature, as blockages in his endeavors to actualize aspects of this nature.

I have said "understanding" of man. I could say "knowledge of the nature of man" or "concept" or "image of man." But "knowledge" sounds too static, "concept" too intellectual, and "image" too aesthetic. No term is entirely adequate. I choose the term *understanding,* in its etymological sense of "standing under," that is, a basic context in which we can encounter and work with our patients.

I shall take up three central problems in psychotherapy which illustrate and exemplify this need for an understanding of the fundamental nature of man. With each problem I hope to show, first, the difficulties we have got into because we have lacked this understanding; second, how phenomenology, as I understand it, hopefully can give us the norms we need; third, how neurosis is a distortion of these norms; and fourth, some implications which follow therefrom for our psychotherapy.

First, *the problem of defining health, illness and neurosis*. In our fields we have been in the strange position of deducing our image of the normal, healthy man from sickness and neurosis. The people who don't break down don't come for help; and problems of a kind which does not fit our techniques we tend not to perceive. Since we identify neurosis (and many forms of psychosis) only by virtue of the fact that the sufferers therefrom cannot fit into our society, and since we understand illness by virtue of our techniques, we are bound to end up with a view of man which is a mirror of our culture and our techniques. This inevitably results in a *progressively empty* view of man. Health becomes the vacuum which is left when the so-called neurosis is cured. On the psychosis level, if a man can stay out of jail and support himself, we call that vacuum health.

This empty view of health (filled only by some vague biological assumptions about "growth," "satisfactions of libido," and so forth) has had much to do with the general tendencies in our day toward ennui, passionlessness, emotional and spiritual emptiness. The empty view of health often puts psychiatry and psychology, as well as other forms of science, on the side of making life increasingly more possible and longer at the price of making existence more boring. From this point of view we can understand why our patients often show a strange lack of zest for getting better, for they may not be so irrational in suspecting that neurosis is more interesting than health, and that health may be the royal road to apathy.

This negative, progressively empty view of health—which I believe is implied in classical psychoanalysis as well as other disciplines —led inevitably to a swing to a frankly *social-conformist* definition of health. In this the norms of health are drawn from the requirements of the culture. This is the distortion, and the sometimes real error, of "cultural" schools like Horney's and my interpersonal school: they hover dangerously on the edge of conformism, the next step in which is "the organization man." I do not mean that this is what Freud or Horney or Sullivan at all intended. I mean that the lack of an adequate concept of the nature of man has made the definition of health inevitably empty, and into that vacuum rush such imposters as "adjustment," "fitting in," "according one's self with the realities of the society," and so on. This tendency, I believe, increases radically with the recent emergence of "operant conditioning" forms of psychotherapy which are based on an outspoken denial of any need for a theory of man at all beyond the therapist's assumption that whatever goals he himself and his society have chosen are the best for all possible men.

How can phenomenology help us with respect to our concept of health? When a patient comes in and sits down in the chair opposite me in my consulting room, what can I assume about him? I shall offer some principles which have been helpful to me,[2] which I have already touched upon, but shall develop further here. I assume that this person, like all beings, is centered in himself, and an attack on this centeredness is an attack on his existence. He is here in my office because this centeredness has broken down or is precariously threatened. Neurosis, then, is seen not as a deviation from my particular theories of what a person ought to be, but precisely as the method the individual uses to preserve his own centeredness, his own existence. His symptoms are his way of shrinking the range of his world in order that his centeredness may be protected from threat; a way of blocking off aspects of his environment that he may be adequate to the remainder. We now see why the definition of neurosis as a "failure of adjustment" is inadequate. An adjustment is exactly what a neurosis is; and that is just its trouble. It is a necessary adjustment by which centeredness can be preserved; a way of accepting non-being in order that some little being may be preserved. *Neurosis, or illness of various sorts, is the distortion of this need for centeredness.*

Let us note already the relation of this concept of centeredness to Husserl's phenomenology. I was fortunate to be able to discuss these problems with my colleague Professor Dorian Cairns of the New School for Social Research, translator of Husserl's *Cartesian Medita-*

tions. Professor Cairns pointed out that my principle of centeredness has its parallel in Husserl's emphasis on *integration.* Husserl believed that inherent in man, and in mind as such, is the "drive" toward consistency, the need for the increasing of experience and the integration of this experience. Thus life is not simply a random, haphazard series of events and observations, but has form and potential meaning. Mental activity is *protentive.*

THE SECOND PROBLEM I wish to cite on which psychotherapy needs the aid of phenomenology is the relationship between the two people, patient and therapist, in the consulting room. This refers to what is called transference in classical analysis. The concept and description of transference was one of Freud's great contributions, both in his own judgment and in that of many of the rest of us. There are vast implications for therapy in the phenomenon that the patient brings into the consulting room his previous or present relationships with father, mother, lover, child, and proceeds to perceive us as those creatures and build his world with us in the same way as he does with them. Transference, like other concepts of Freud, vastly enlarges the sphere and influence of personality; we live in others and they in us. Note Freud's idea that for each partner in every act of sexual intercourse four persons are present—one's self and one's lover, plus one's two parents. I have always personally taken an ambivalent attitude toward this idea, believing as I do that the act of love at least deserves some privacy. But the deeper implications are the fateful interweaving of the human web; one's ancestors, like Hamlet's father, are always coming on to the edge of the stage with various ghostly challenges and imprecations. This emphasis of Freud's on how deeply we are bound each to each again cuts through many of modern man's illusions about love and interpersonal relations.

But the concept of transference presents us with unending difficulties if we take it by itself, i.e., without a norm of relationship which is grounded in the nature of man as such. In the first place, transference can be a handy and ever-useful defense for the therapist, as Thomas Szasz puts it; the therapist can hide behind it to protect himself from the anxiety of direct encounter. Secondly, the concept of transference can undermine the whole experience and sense of reality in therapy; the two persons in the consulting room become "shadows," and everyone else in the world does too. It can erode the patient's sense of responsibility and can rob the therapy of much of the dynamic for the patient's change.

What has been lacking is a concept of *encounter,* within which, and only within which, transference has genuine meaning. *Transference is to be understood as the distortion of encounter.* Since there was no norm of human encounter in psychoanalysis and no adequate place for the I-Thou relationship, there was bound to be an oversimplifying and watering down of love relationships. Freud greatly deepened our understanding of the multifarious, powerful and ubiquitous forms in which erotic drives express themselves. But eros (instead of coming back into its own, as Freud fondly hoped) now oscillates between being an absurd chemistry that demands outlet and a relatively unimportant pastime for male and female when they get bored watching TV of an evening.

Also we had no norm of *agape* in its own right. Agape cannot be understood as derivative, or as what is left over when you analyze our exploitative, cannibalistic tendencies. Agape is not a sublimation of eros but a transcending of it in enduring tenderness, lasting concern for others; and it is precisely this transcendence which gives eros itself fuller and more enduring meaning.

The phenomenological approach helps us in asking the question, How is it possible that one being can relate to another? What is the nature of human beings that *Mitsein* is possible, that two men can communicate, can each grasp the other as a being, have genuine concern for the welfare and fulfillment of the other, and experience some genuine trust? The answer to these questions will tell us *of what* transference is a distortion.

As I sit now in relationship with my patient, the principle I continue to assume is: this being, like all existing beings, has the need and possibility of going out from his centeredness to participate in other beings. Before this man ever made the tentative and oft-postponed steps to phone me for an appointment, he was already participating in imagination in some relationship with me. He sat nervously smoking in my waiting room; he now looks at me with mingled suspicion and hope, an effort toward openness fighting in him against the life-old tendency to withdraw behind a stockade and hold me out. This struggle is understandable, for *participating always involves risk:* if he, or any organism, goes out too far, he will lose his own centeredness, his identity. But if he is so afraid of losing his own conflicted center—which at least has made possible some partial integration and meaning in his experience—that he refuses to go out at all but holds back in rigidity and lives in narrowed and shrunken world space, his growth and development are blocked. This was the common neurotic pattern in Freud's day and is what Freud referred to when he spoke of repression and inhibition. Inhibition is the relation to the world of the being who has the possibility of going out but is too threatened to do so; and his fear that he will lose too much may, of course, correspond literally to the facts of the case.[3]

But in our day of conformism and the outer-directed man, the most prevalent neurotic pattern takes the opposite form, namely, going out too far, dispersing one's self in participation and identification with others until one's own being is emptied. This is no longer the issue of transference, but is the psychocultural phenomenon of the organization man. It is one reason too, it seems to me, that castration is no longer the dominant fear of men or women in our day, but ostracism. Patient after patient I have seen (especially patients from Madison Avenue) chooses to be castrated, that is, to give up his power, in order not to be ostracized. The real threat is not to be accepted, to be thrown out of the group, to be left solitary and alone. In this overparticipation, one's own consistency becomes inconsistent because it fits someone else. One's own meaning becomes meaningless because it is borrowed from somebody else's meaning.

SPEAKING NOW more concretely of the contempt of encounter, I mean it to refer to the fact that in the therapeutic hour a total relationship is going on between two people which involves a number of different levels. One level is that of real persons: I am glad to see my patient (varying on different days depending chiefly on the amount of sleep I have had the night before). Our seeing each other allays the physical loneliness to which all human beings are heir. Another level is that of *friends:* we trust—for we have seen each other a lot—that the other has some genuine concern for listening and understanding. Another level is that of *esteem* or *agape,* the capacity which I think inheres in Mitwelt of self-transcending concern for another's welfare. Another level will be frankly *erotic.* When I was doing supervision with her some years ago, Clara Thompson once said to me something I've often pondered, that if one person in the therapeutic relationship feels active erotic attraction, the other will too. Erotic feelings of his own need to be frankly faced by the therapist; otherwise he will, at least in fantasy, act out his own needs with the patient. But more important, unless he accepts the erotic as one of the ways of communication, he will not listen for what he should hear from the patient and he will lose one of the most dynamic resources for change in therapy.

Now this total encounter, which I have said can be our most useful medium of understanding the patient as well as our most efficacious instrument for helping him open himself to the possibility of change, seems to me often to have the resonant character of two musical instruments. If you pluck a violin string, the corresponding strings in another violin in the room will resonate with similar movement of their own. This is an analogy, of course: what goes on in human beings includes that but is much more complex.

Encounter in human beings is always to a greater or lesser extent *anxiety-creating* as well as *joy-creating.* I think these effects arise out of the fact that genuine encounter with another person always shakes our self-world relationship: our comfortable temporary security of the moment before is thrown into question, we are opened, made tentative for an instant—shall we risk ourselves, take the chance to be enriched by this new relationship (and even if it is a friend or loved one of long standing, this particular moment of relationship is still new)? Or shall we brace ourselves, throw up a stockade, hold out the other person and miss the nuances of his perceptions, feelings, intentions? Encounter is always a potentially creative experience; it normally should ensue in the expanding of consciousness, the enrichment of the self. (I do not speak here of *quantity*—obviously a brief meeting may affect us only slightly; I refer rather to a *quality* of experience.) In genuine encounter both persons are changed, however minutely. C. G. Jung has pointed out rightly that in effective therapy a change occurs in *both* the therapist and the patient; unless the therapist is open to change the patient will not be either.

The phenomenon of encounter very much needs to be studied, for it seems clear that much more is going on than almost any of us has realized. I propose the hypothesis that in therapy, granted adequate clarification of the therapist, *it is not possible for one person to have a feeling without the other having it to some degree also.* I know you will see many exceptions to this, but I want to offer the thesis to ponder and work on. One corollary of my hypothesis is that in Mitwelt there is necessarily some resonance, and that the reason we don't feel it, when we don't, is some blocking on our part. Frieda Fromm-Reichmann often used to say that her best instrument for telling what the patient feels—e.g., anxiety or fear or love or anger that he, the patient, dare not express—is what she feels within herself. This use of one's self as the instrument of course requires a tremendous self-discipline on the part of the therapist. I don't mean at all here to open the door simply to telling the patient what you feel; your feelings may be neurotic in all sorts of ways, and the patient has enough problems without being further burdened with yours. I mean rather that the self-discipline, the self-purification if you will, the bracketing of one's own distortions and neurotic tendencies to the extent a therapist is able, seems to me to result in his being in greater or lesser degree able to experience encounter as a way of participating in the feelings and the world of the patient. All this needs to be studied, and I believe can be, in many more ways than we have realized. As I have said, I am convinced that there is something going on in one human being relating to another, something inhering in Mitwelt, that is infinitely more complex, subtle, rich, and powerful than we have generally realized.

The chief reason these nuances I have been talking about have not been studied is that we have had no concept of encounter. Since Freud we have had a clear concept of transference; and as one consequence, we have had all kinds of studies of transference—which tell us everything except what really goes on between two human beings. To those philosophers who feel that pure phenomenology is being polluted by the psychotherapists, may I say that what we are trying to do as psychotherapists is to get some understanding of man that will enable us at least to see what is going on, and then to study it. We are justified in looking to phenomenology for help in arriving at such a concept as will enable us to perceive encounter itself, when so far we have only perceived its distortion, transference. It is especially important, let me add, that we not yield to the tendency in our professions to avoid and dilute encounter by making it a derivative of transference or countertransference.

The third problem is that of "the unconscious." This is a particularly knotty problem in relation to phenomenology. We all know the difficulties inherent in the "cellar" theory of the unconscious—the concept that it is a level below ground where all sorts of entities are stored. And we know how this concept of the unconscious can be used as a blank check on which every kind of cause-and-effect determinism can be written. The negative use of the unconscious is summed up beautifully in a sentence by my friend Erwin Straus: "The unconscious thoughts of the patient are generally the conscious theories of the therapist." Obviously the "cellar" view of the unconscious must be rejected.

But the arguments of Sartre and the other phenomenologists rejecting the unconscious in any form, logical as such arguments are, have always struck me as legalistic and verbalistic. One of Sartre's arguments is that Freud's censor, which is supposed to stand at the gate of the unconscious and decide which thoughts can get through to consciousness, must "know" a great deal; it must "know" what the id knows as well as what can be permitted to come into consciousness. This I accept. But Sartre is only describing here another aspect of the fact that the ways of the mind are complex and subtle indeed. I would agree that any experience of which we are unconscious is to some extent present in awareness, or at least potentially so. The real problem is why the person cannot let himself "know that he knows this." There is no doubt whatever, in my judgment, of the existence and importance of the phenomena Freud was trying to describe when he talked about the unconscious. If we throw this hypothesis overboard, we will the more impoverish ourselves by losing a great deal of the richness and significance of human experience.

How then are we to meet the issue? I find two principles helpful to me here, one having to do with awareness and the other with consciousness. The distinction between these two is critical for our problem. I will state them, beginning with awareness, in reference to my original concept of centeredness, namely, the subjective side of centeredness is awareness. Awareness is a capacity we share with animals and much of nature. Indeed Whithead and Tillich in their respective ontologies hold that awareness is characteristic of all things in nature, down to the attraction and repulsion between the molecular particles.

Awareness is often correlated in our patients with acting out and paranoid behavior. It is possible, that is, to be aware without being conscious. We all know the intelligent, often compulsive patient who can talk for hours with great awareness about what is going on in his life relationships but with no experience whatever that he himself is in on the relationships. I listened in a supervision group recently to a tape of a well-educated man who had been in analysis for nine years, who talked at great length and very astutely about the mechanisms his wife was using in their relationships and about the mechanisms between the two; but what struck me was his complete lack of awareness that he was the other half of the relationship. I felt as though I were in a ghostly room hearing a voice but with no person there. Awareness without consciousness is highly depersonalizing.

Thus another principle is not only relevant but necessary. I state it as follows: Consciousness is the distinctly human form of awareness—the particularly human capacity not only to know something but to know that I know it, that is, to experience myself as subject in relation to an object or as I in relation to Thou. I find Erwin Straus's work such as the perdurable paper, "The Upright Posture," pertinent and basic for the distinction between awareness and consciousness. The animal who walks on all fours, like the chow dog in our family, has immeasurably greater awareness in many ways than I have. Our dog's alertness at a great distance through his senses of smell and hearing is a source of endless amazement and makes me feel we human being are indeed pretty poor specimens from an evolutionary point of view. On our farm this dog can detect other animals or persons coming in the gate far down the road, and being a chow, he assumes that those not of our family are of course to be eaten up without further ado.

But when man rises on two legs, stands upright, and sees, he does not sense *at* a distance but is aware *of* a distance between himself and the world. This distance I believe is correlated with consciousness. Dr. Plessner's paper "On Human Expression" has much to say of significance on this point.[4] The same phenomenon is what makes "Man, the Questioning Being." [5] We could not question without being aware of the distance between us and the world. Questioning implies that I stand in some significant relationship to the world and thus is a distinguishing expression of consciousness.

Now I come back to the problem of the unconscious. How shall we interpret unconscious phenomena which are so richly evident in dreams, so significantly present in the whole spectrum of feelings and actions of our patients and ourselves? We must redefine the concept at the outset. One cannot say *the* unconscious, for it is never a place. Nor are *things* in the sense of entities unconscious; things are not repressed; rather, mental processes and potentialities are. I propose as a definition the following: *Unconscious experience is the potentialities for action and awareness which the person cannot or will not actualize.* These potentialities may be nevertheless actualized bodily; denied sexual desires and potentialities are expressed in somatic symptoms, as Freud so well knew. But the important point is that the individual will not or cannot let himself be conscious of the desire.

It is critically important, as I have already indicated, to keep the distinction between awareness and consciousness. The patient may well have been "aware" on some level of the experience which is denied and therefore of which he is unconscious. Thus when he says, "I knew it all the time," his point is correct. But his term is wrong: he may well have been *aware* of the repressed experience, but he could not let himself *know that he knew it.*

I think when Sartre argues that the censor knew it all the time, he is talking about awareness and not consciousness. The concept "unconscious" is to be understood on the basis of and derived from "conscious," and not the other way around, as the evolutionary thinkers are prone to do. If one wishes to talk in evolutionary terms, one should say that consciousness and the capacity to deny it, namely, the unconscious, emerge from an undifferentiated awareness. Unconsciousness is a description of the infinite and protean forms of consciousness.

Now it is often argued that phenomenology, particularly in its Husserlian form, has to do solely with consciousness. This is not entirely true. Professor Cairns stated his opinion in discussion with me, that it is "as if" Husserl left a place for unconsciousness by confining himself to the description of consciousness. It was also Professor Cairns' opinion that my redefinitions of unconsciousness are, at least to some extent, compatible with Husserl's phenomenology as he understands it.

The implications for therapy of this analysis of unconscious experience are significant. It was said by Freud that the task of the analyst is to make the unconscious conscious. I would put it, rather, that the task of the therapist is to help the patient transmute awareness into consciousness. This process involves all the potentialities which I have described as unconscious, but they are to some extent present in awareness, or at least potentially so. Consciousness consists of the experience, "I am the one who has this world, and am doing something in it." This implies responsibility, *"responding to"* the world.

Thus in transmuting awareness into consciousness, we have a dynamic for change, i.e., increasing the patient's sphere of consciousness and experience, which inheres directly in the patient's own being. The urge and movement for change and fulfillment does not have to be brought in from the outside, by Victorian voluntarism or by conditioning or by modern conformist moralizing. It comes directly out of the patient's own being and his need to fulfill that being.

NOTES FOR CHAPTER 7

1. It was Freud's ever present mythology, like the Oedipus myth, and his ever ready ability and courage to *think* mythologically which saved him from the full mechanistic implications of his determinism. The image of man he sought—i.e., one fitting the deterministic categories of natural science of the nineteenth century—he never succeeded in achieving because his mythology always broke in to bring new dimensions to the image. (A similar thing happens in a different context when Plato tries to think logically about man; at the end of logical categories, Plato's thinking goes into orbit on the wings of a myth.) But when Freudianism crosses the Atlantic Ocean, the mythology is the first thing thrown overboard. Thus the mechanism and determinism of Freudianism becomes a more difficult and stultifying problem in this country than in Europe; it makes bedfellows of behaviorism on one side and logical positivism on the other.

2. I call these principles ontological, following Paul Tillich, to whom I am indebted for their philosophical formulation. This paragraph is a re-statement of a section from a previous paper in which I have tried to work out these principles in greater detail, "Existential Bases of Psychotherapy," in *Existential Psychology,* edited by Rollo May, Random House, New York, 1961.

3. Patients will say, "If I love somebody, it's as though all of me flows out like water out of a river, and there'll be nothing left." I think this is a very accurate *statement of transference.* That is, if one's love is something that does not belong there of its own right, then obviously it will be emptied; the whole matter is one of economic balance, as Freud put it.

4. Helmuth Plessner, "On Human Expression," in Erwin Straus, ed., *Phenomenology: Pure and Applied,* Duquesne University Press, Pittsburgh, 1964.

5. Erwin Straus, *Phenomenological Psychology,* Basic Books, New York, 1966.

8

Existential Therapy and the American Scene

And freely men confesse that this world's spent,
When in the Planets, and the Firmament
They seek so many new; . . .
'Tis all in peeces, all cohaerence gone;
All just supply, and all Relation:
Prince, Subject, Father, Sonne, are things forgot,
For every man alone thinkes he hath got
To be a Phoenix. . . .
—JOHN DONNE (*1573-1631*), An Anatomie of the World, *"The First Anniversary"*

Our problem is set by a paradox which confronts us as soon as we state the topic of existential analysis and the American scene. On one hand, existential analysis has many profound and important affinities with underlying traits in the American character. But American psychology and psychiatry have been decidedly ambivalent toward it. In asking the reasons for this curious contradiction, we must not hide behind the fact that translations of the basic works of existential psychiatrists and psychologists have not been available in America (or in English) until half a dozen years ago; for translations follow interest rather than simply interest following translations.

In this chapter I wish, first, to show the relationship between some major tenets of existential psychotherapy and underlying traits in American character and thought. Second, I wish to point out some aspects of our American situation which cast light on the paradox that though we are in some ways a very existential people, we are suspicious of existentialism. Third, I want to emphasize some elements in existential analysis which some of us have found of special significance in our psychotherapy. And fourth, I propose to cite several unsolved problems and criticisms of existential analysis posed by American psychotherapists.

A central emphasis running through the existential approach, namely, the emphasis on *knowing by doing,* is particularly close to American thought. When Kierkegaard proclaims, "Truth exists for the individual only as he himself produces it in action," the words have a familiar ring to those of us brought up in the American pragmatic tradition. Paul Tillich, a philosopher who represents one wing of existential thought, has excellently expressed in his book, *The Courage to Be,*[1] the latent existential attitude of multitudes of Americans. In his classical paper on existential philosophy, Tillich wrote:

> Like the American philosophers William James and John Dewey, the existential philosophers are appealing from the conclusions of "Rationalistic" thinking which equates Reality with the object of thought, with relations or "essences," to Reality as men experience it immediately in their actual living. They consequently take their place with all those who have regarded man's immediate experience as revealing more completely the nature and traits of Reality than man's cognitive experience.[2]

Also very important in American thought and attitudes are the distrust of abstract categories or theorizing for its own sake, a distrust shown so strongly by Kierkegaard, and the rejection of the subject-object dichotomy.

If one reads William James, particularly, one finds amazing kinship with the existential thinkers. Beyond the points cited above, James shows a *passionate emphasis on immediacy of experience.* He held that no one can know truth by sitting in a detached armchair, but only in experience which includes *willing.* That is to say, *decision* in one's self is a necessary preliminary to the opening up of truth. His epistemology has striking similarities to that of Nietzsche in the first part of the *Will to Power,* when Nietzsche holds that truth is the way a biological group actualizes itself. Finally, William

James had a great humaneness and through his own vast breadth as a man was able to bring art and religion into his thought without sacrificing any of his scientific integrity. He almost single-handed saved American psychology at the turn of the century from becoming lost in armchair philosophizing on one hand or the minutiae of the physiopsychological laboratory on the other. He is in many ways our most typical American thinker.

But by the same paradox we discussed above, William James was generally dismissed with mild contempt in American universities in the period between the two world wars. Psychology and psychiatry in the last three decades have by and large been behavioristic and positivistic. James is representative of the underlying attitudes in America which are just below the conscious surface, and it is highly significant that a rebirth of interest in him and appreciation of his great importance as a thinker is now occurring in our universities. In a parallel way, the interest in existential analysis in America has been latent and suppressed, held just beneath the conscious surface of American thought.

What is the source of this paradox? I invite you to glance with me at certain dilemmas in our American situation which throw light upon it. Western man's preoccupation with mechanistic methods and his apotheosis of technique have fallen particularly hard upon us in America; and in some ways our conflicts reflect the most critical and portentous dilemmas of Western man.

I propose that the best way to understand the American character is to see it via the symbol of the *frontier*. Most of us are literally just one or two generations from the frontier, from the actual pioneer state. And even if, like children of immigrant families, we were not brought up on the geographical frontier, we are still only one generation from the economic or educational frontier. On the frontier it was essential that you emphasize *practice,* that you be able to clear your own land and build your own house. Individual self-reliance was of first importance, for the individual man and his family often had to live by themselves in isolated places in prairies and forests. It is easy to see how subjectivity and introspection would be a real threat to these physically isolated people, and how they needed to repress their subjectivity radically to escape breakdown. Hence our suspicion of theorizing, abstract speculation, or intellectualizing for its own sake.

The frontier furthermore was always mobile; there was always some place to go horizontally. The individual did not need, as in Europe, to go vertically into his own experience. Hence the great emphasis on *space* and *spatial* categories in America, in contrast to the European interest in *time*. The American courage in changing jobs—what the sociologists call economic motility—is not at all to be understood as merely a crass materialism or solely a hunger for economic gain: it shows a self-reliance midway between material and spiritual poles. As Paul Tillich points out, it is a spiritual attitude of courage to risk one's self, to take one's destiny into one's own hands. This is associated with the conviction in America that everybody can change his life, sometimes called our "optimistic existentialism." Hence the great concern in America with helping people with their problems. The vast spread of marriage clinics, adjustment centers, and the widespread popularity of psychotherapy are partly connected with this conviction that everyone should be able to become something new.

Could not the question be fruitfully raised whether our emphasis on pragmatic rationalism and practical controls, and our behavioristic ways of thinking, are not a defense against the irrational elements which were present in most of our society only a hundred years ago on the frontiers? These irrational elements are always bursting out, often to our considerable embarrassment—from the revivalistic prairie fires of emotional movements of the nineteenth century to the Ku Klux Klan and the anti-intellectual movement itself. A good deal of our psychological work can be seen as efforts to control this irrationalism.

But I think there is a special point here about our concern and preoccupation in the United States with "behavior." Our sciences of man are called "behavioral sciences"; the American Psychological Association's national television programs are called "Accent on *Behavior*" and our chief, and most extensive, original contribution to Western psychological development is *behaviorism*. Practically all of us in our society heard all the time as children, "Behave yourselves! . . . Behave, behave!" Is not our emphasis on behavior also a carry-over of our frontiersmen's puritanism? The hypothesis of the close relation between our inherited moralistic puritanism and our preoccupation with behavior in our study of man, culminating in our "behavior sciences," is by no means absurd, and the study of this thesis could yield some interesting results. I am, of course, entirely aware of the argument that we have to study behavior because that's all we have available in any kind of objectivity. But is this not our parochial prejudice, very much determined by our particular historical time, raised to the level of a scientific principle?

The frontier virtues in the American character carried with them serious dangers, and here is where the paradox of the suppression of the existential attitude becomes clearer. For the emphasis on "practice" and spatial motility led to overemphasis on *techniques,* the worship of technique as a mechanical way of controlling nature, and to the corollary need therefore to see human personality as an object of control like the rest of nature. At this point the peculiar tragedy of Western man takes its special toll in America. Belief in technique can be an effective anxiety-allaying method; and it may well be that we in America have reacted to the upsets of the contemporary catastrophic situation in Western society chiefly with that method. This belief goes with the frantic though illusory hope that somehow we shall not have to face the devastating anxiety of the present world predicament if we can only find the right technique.

The virtues cited above have likewise played into an overoptimism about human nature, an optimism which understandably though unfortunately became married to the faith in techniques. One of our serious dangers in America is the tendency to believe that technique *in itself* changes people, that anyone can change if only he finds the right method. This faith oftentimes may serve as a substitute for courage inwardly to confront one's own existence in its tragic as well as joyous possibilities. *To do* is often easier, and may allay anxiety more quickly, than *to be.*

A further problem arises from the fact that on the frontier every man started from scratch. Every man in theory constructed his own history. Hence we tend to lack a sense of history as well as the deeper experiences of *time* in being. But most serious of all, in my judgment, is our lack of the sense of the tragedy in human existence.

Gabriel Marcel has said that the characteristic of modern Western man is his *repression of the ontological sense,* his running away from the awareness of his own being. Marcel rightly suggests that it is precisely this ontological repression, rather than repression of instincts, which underlies the deepest aspects of modern Western man's neurosis. The repression of the ontological sense, for example, is what we really mean by the somewhat vague expression "loss of being a person" and lies behind the vast movements of conformism and the tendencies toward loss of individual self-consciousness in our day. Many Americans are deeply concerned about this repression of the ontological sense, for our good fortune itself makes us particularly vulnerable to this loss. Our vast resources and our geographical position have enabled us to avoid the tragic shocks to existence that have forced peoples in Europe to be concerned with ontology whether they wish to be or not and have forced them directly to confront anxiety, death, and the other existential dilemmas of life.

Now we arrive at exactly the point where a most significant change is occurring in America. There is a strong emerging attitude in American thought of what I would call "ontological hunger." This was shown in its popular form in the widespread religious revival in the 1950's. But it is also shown in the questions of existential meaning asked by scientists and cultural leaders of all sorts in America. About the religious revival I, for one, had grave doubts because of its conformist character. But there can be no doubt of the significance of the new concern among psychiatrists and psychologists and other intellectuals about the meaning of human existence. Though I suspect that the positivistic emphasis in American psychiatry and psychology will be dominant for some time to come, there are clear signs that the existential emphasis will have a profound influence as a yeast, a leaven in the loaf.

Some of the particular aspects of existential psychiatry and psychology which we, therefore, find of special value and significance are these. First, the passionate insistence that man be treated even in science as more than *homo naturans,* and the insistence that the distinctive conditions of man's humanity are our special concern— an emphasis so central in Binswanger's work. Second, the breaking through of the "epistemological loneliness" of our modern situation, and the undermining of the narrow, outmoded Western causality— a phenomenological contribution made with such elegance and clarity in the phenomenology of Minkowski and Straus. Third, the emphasis that every psychotherapy is based upon philosophical presuppositions, and that only harm and confusion can come from obscuring these presuppositions. I agree with Zilboorg's caution against tying psychotherapy too closely to any particular philosophy. The crucial point, in my judgment, however, is different from Dr. Zilboorg's. My contention is that most psychotherapeutic schools have not admitted they need any philosophy at all—they need only "objectively look at the facts," blissfully unaware that this very process of looking at the facts involves most radical and profound philosophical assumptions. It is essential that we clarify the *ontological* bases on which the dynamisms of psychoanalysis rest. I cannot overemphasize the importance of this enterprise, for I think such dynamisms as transference, resistance, and so forth, hang in the air and can have no lasting meaning except as their ontological basis, in man's situation as man, can be understood.[3]

I believe, furthermore, that the existential approach can and should have profound and far-reaching effects on practical therapy with patients, though this contribution has not as yet been adequately developed. The existential approach should break through the artificiality of much traditional psychotherapy and bring a more dynamic sense of reality into the process. Psychotherapy will then not be *treatment* in the narrow sense, but will be an encounter with one's own existence in an immediate and quintessential form. A specific aspect of this new dynamic, for one example, is seen in the principle that *decision precedes insight and knowledge.* It used to be assumed that when the patient got enough insight, he would make the right decisions. Now we see that this is only a half-truth and actually invites the patient to surrender his own existence. The other and entirely necessary half of the truth is that the patient will never get insights, never be able to see the truth, *except as he is ready to come to decisions about his own existence.* The significance of the personal relation between therapist and patient is not merely that it gives the patient a new, and now good, father or mother, but more basically that it gives the patient a new personal world, characterized by stable concern, in which he becomes able to take a decisive orientation to his own existence.

The existential emphasis, furthermore, changes the goals of therapy. We are now no longer seduced by the ubiquitous idea of adjustment, which in our society can too often be only a name for conformism and actual loss of one's own existence. The goal is rather the full confronting of one's own existence even though one may then be *less* adjusted to society, and even though one may well carry *more* conscious anxiety, that is, normal existential anxiety, than before. This shift of goals enables us to deal with the most important realities of life which have generally had only a shadowy position in therapy heretofore, namely, *normal* anxiety and guilt, joy, love, and creativity.

I wish now to cite several problems and criticisms which impress me. The first has to do with the denial in much existential and phenomenological psychiatry of what is called "the unconscious." I propose modestly to accuse many of our existential colleagues, particularly in Europe, of being *unexistential* in dealing with "the unconscious." Now it is true, as we have seen, that the concept of the unconscious in psychoanalysis has played notoriously into the tendency toward oversimplified mechanistic causation. But our reaction to this should lead us, not to a denial, but to a new formulation of the deeper and vaster realms of experience symbolized by the concept of the unconscious. Therapists and patients often talk of something in the patient's unconscious "causing" this or that symptom or behavior. This is the "cellar" idea of unconscious experience, and of course should be rejected.

But the real historical meaning of Freud's formulation of the unconscious has a quite different significance. Its great meaning is an *enlargement* of the dimensions of personality, a breaking through the narrow rationalism and voluntarism of Victorian man. The idea of unconscious experience gives personality depth dimensions that Victorian culture sought to deny, the depths of what we call the irrational, the primitive, the repressed or forgotten ideas, urges, and other aspects of personality which are intimately bound up with many of man's tragic potentialities. This dimension is the historical meaning of the emergence of this concept of unconscious experience among the existential thinkers of the eighteenth century, Schopenhauer and Nietzsche, and in Eduard von Hartmann, whose book Freud read. Though Freud himself errs in using this concept in the blank check, oversimplified way, his real genius is shown in the broader meaning of the term, namely the radical enlargement of the depth dimensions of human personality. In my judgment many of the arguments of existential and phenomenological writers against "the unconscious" are themselves too legalistic, dealing in verbal logic, and fail to take the term in its dynamic, existential meaning. Surely, it is always inaccurate to speak of *the* unconscious, *the* preconscious or subconscious: these are never *places*. But we must be able to include *unconscious experience*. This is a problem not yet adequately dealt with. I look forward, paradoxical as it may sound, to someone's contributing to us a *phenomenology of unconscious experience*.

The second problem is the underemphasis in much existential analysis on the genetic dimension. I am entirely aware of the abuses of genetic causality in psychoanalysis, shown in the tendencies to say a patient does something *because* this or that happened to him in childhood. It is a real danger, especially in America, that we become so interested in immediately asking *why* a person behaves in this or that way that we never understand *what* he is doing. Certainly this oversimplified causality short-circuits the genuine understanding of the patient. Nevertheless, we cannot doubt the great formative power of early childhood experiences. Such experiences are not causal in the oversimplified way but they have a quintessence of power that is expressed later in symbols; they are formative forces of what Adler called the "style of life." A renowned colleague of mine remarked recently that there is a danger that phenomenology may become only two-dimensional. Is it not evident that the existence of an individual can never be seen in its fullness without the dimension of historical genesis, and that a way must be found to bring in the richness and dynamic of childhood experiences on a different basis from the old causality?

A third problem my colleagues raise is the lack of therapeutic interest in some European existential psychiatric writing. I may be accused here of the old American preoccupation with applied science, our wanting to change everybody. I make no apologies for our concern with helping anyone who suffers, quixotic though that may seem at times. My point here, however, is more than that. For you never can grasp the other person in his real existence unless you see him at every instant in process of trying to become something. His self, as Kierkegaard insisted, is only that which he is in process of becoming. Moral growth and change is an ever present aspect of the living experience—and a person's denying this moral change only proves it from a different angle. Furthermore, we can find people revealed only in critical situations; no person will go through the agonies of baring the deepest aspects of his psychological and spiritual suffering except as he has some hope of gaining help in finding his way out of his agony. Psychology and psychiatry, I propose, are two sciences which cannot know their material, i.e., persons, except as they are oriented directly or indirectly to helping these persons.

NOTES FOR CHAPTER 8

1. Paul Tillich, *The Courage to Be,* Yale University Press, New Haven, 1952.
2. Tillich, "Existential Philosophy," *Journal of the History of Ideas,* 5:1, 44-70, 1944. I do not of course mean to equate American pragmatism and existentialism. I mean only to say that they have several emphases in common, such as the rejection of the subject-object dichotomy, the denial of the identification of logical categories with truth, etc.
3. We made one endeavor to do this in Chapter 7.

9

Jean-Paul Sartre and Psychoanalysis

> ORESTES: *Let it crumble! Let the rocks revile me, and*
> *flowers wilt at my coming. Your whole universe is*
> *not enough to prove me wrong. You are the king of*
> *gods, king of stones and stars, king of the waves of*
> *the sea. But you are not the king of men.*
>
> ZEUS: *Impudent spawn! So I am not your king? Who,*
> *then, made you?*
>
> ORESTES: *You. But you blundered; you should not have*
> *made me free.*
>
> —JEAN-PAUL SARTRE, The Flies

I have two contrasting viewpoints with respect to the work of Sartre. One is that his thought needs to be taken with genuine seriousness as one of the unquestionably important contributions in our time to modern Western man's self-interpretation in philosophy, psychology, and literature. My other belief is that some of Sartre's underlying principles are basically mistaken. And it also seems to me that to take into account both these viewpoints is the most constructive and fruitful way for Sartre to be approached by college students and other thoughtful modern people.

To appreciate Sartre's contribution we must, of course, first dissociate him from the superficial interpretations of his ideas by the extremists of the Café Deux Magots and the left bank of the Seine and the Hudson. True, Sartre himself has invited such misinterpretations with his superficially rash statements like that which ends Chapter III of *Existential Psychoanalysis*—"Man is a useless passion." But "useless" here can be taken as meaning "not to be used."

Behind the nihilistic implications of some of his terms, there really lies Sartre's passionate and perdurable insistence that man is not an object to be *used*, whether by God or by psychiatry or psychology, or manipulated by the giant computers of modern industrialism or fashioned into a mechanical passive consumer by mass communication.

Nor is man to be used by way of his own manipulation of himself as a psychological machine to be adjusted, or molded by Norman Vincent Peale's "positive thinking" into an organization man to win success on Madison Avenue. Man is not an object to be forced into the "role demanded by modern society—to be *only* a waiter or a conductor or a mother, *only* an employer or a worker," as Miss Hazel Barnes writes in her introduction to her translation of Sartre.[1] She goes on rightly to say, "To my mind this aspect of Sartre's existentialism is one of his most positive and most important contributions—the attempt to make contemporary man look for himself again and refuse to be absorbed in a role on the stage of a puppet theater."

All through these pages the reader will find Sartre's sharp attacks on the contemporary psychology which sees man as an object for conditioning or holds that "the individual is only the intersection of universal schemata."[2] Sartre writes that if we "consider man as capable of being analyzed and reduced to original data, to determined drives (or 'desires'), supported by the subject as properties of an object," we may indeed end up with an imposing system of substances which we then call mechanisms or dynamisms or patterns. But we inescapably find ourselves up against a dilemma. Our human being has become "a sort of indeterminate clay which would have to receive [the desires] passively—or he would be reduced to a simple bundle of these irreducible drives or tendencies. In either case the *man* disappears; we can no longer find 'the one' to whom this or that experience has happened."[3]

Sartre thus presents us with a most emphatic statement of human freedom and individual responsibility. "I *am* my choices," he proclaims again and again in various forms. In his dramas he asserts this principle continually and powerfully: Orestes, the chief character in *The Flies,* shouts out against a manipulating and dilettante Zeus, "I *am* my freedom!" Undaunted by Zeus's reminders of the great despair and anxiety which dog the steps of the free man, Orestes cries, "Human life begins on the far side of despair!" In his seeing freedom as the central and unique potentiality that constitutes man as the human being, Sartre gives the most extreme statement of modern existentialism.

But the Sartrean man, it is also true, becomes a solitary, individual creature standing on the base of his defiance alone against God and society. The philosophical basis of this principle is given in Sartre's famous statement, "Freedom is existence, and in it existence precedes essence." That is to say, there would be no *essences*—no truth, no structure in reality, no logical forms, no logos, no God nor any morality—except as man in affirming his freedom makes these truths.

This brings us to what, in my judgment, is the fundamental criticism of Sartre's thought. I wish to present this criticism in the words of Paul Tillich, who sees with balanced wisdom the meaning of the modern existential movement and also Sartre's position in it:

> In contrast to the situation . . . after the second World War, when most people identified existentialism with Sartre, it is now common knowledge in this country that existentialism in the Western intellectual history starts with Pascal in the 17th century, has an underground history in the 18th century, a revolutionary history in the 19th century and an astonishing victory in the 20th century. Existentialism has become the style of our period in all realms of life. Even the analytic philosophers pay tribute to it by withdrawing into formal problems and leaving the field of material problems to the existentialists in art and literature.
>
> There are, however, only rare moments in this monumental development in which an almost pure existentialism has been reached. An example is Sartre's doctrine of man. I refer to a sentence in which the whole problem of essentialism and existentialism comes into the open, his famous statement that man's essence is his existence. The meaning of this sentence is that man is a being of whom no essence can be affirmed, for such an essence would introduce a permanent element, contradictory to man's power of transforming himself indefinitely. According to Sartre, man is what he acts to be.

But if we ask whether his statement has not, against its intention, given an assertion about man's essential nature, we must say, certainly, it has. Man's particular nature is his power to create himself. And if the further question is raised of how such a power is possible and how it must be structured, we need a fully developed essentialist doctrine in order to answer; we must know about his body and his mind, in short, about those questions which for millennia have been discussed in essentialist terms.

Only on the basis of an essentialist doctrine of freedom does Sartre's statement have any meaning. Neither in theology nor in philosophy can existentialism live by itself. It can only exist as a contrasting element within an essentialist framework.[4]

In other words, you cannot have freedom or a free individual without some structure in which (or in the case of defiance, *against* which) the individual acts. Freedom and structure imply each other. And Sartre surely has some structure. In my judgment Sartre presupposes much more of the humanistic tradition of Western thought, and even much more of the Hebrew-Christian concepts of the significance and worth of the person, than he seems to be aware of or explicitly states. He also presupposes the Hebrew-Christian belief in the moral meaning of history. The prophets Amos and Isaiah, for example, cry out against wickedness on the basis of principles of justice to which even God was held accountable. Sartre presupposes similar moral principles in defying such principles. There is an assumption all through Sartre—an assumption owing much to Descartes and French rationalism, and given added conviction by the passionate beliefs of Kierkegaard and Nietzsche—that there is a meaningful structure in life and even in Western bourgeois society to make it possible that such a one as Sartre can fight so powerfully against them. To be an anti-Christ, like Nietzsche, presupposes Christ.

The same thing certainly can be said about Sartre's approach to psychoanalysis. In this volume he presupposes Freud in order to fight tellingly against him. The fact that psychoanalysis is possible at all, that man can overcome psychological problems and that one person (the therapist) can help another (the so-called patient) presupposes a meaningful structure in the human psyche and in human relationships, whether this structure is revealed in dreams, in slips of tongue, in memories of childhood history, in neurotic symptoms, or whatnot. This structure Freud tried to describe and then to systematize. That there are fundamental errors in the system which was the outcome of Freud's endeavor is clear. And I believe Sartre has succeeded in this book in piercing with his sharp and incisive scalpel a number of these errors. But he could not have done so except that he presupposed Freud's essentialist systematic endeavor to start with.

One place where Sartre presupposes Freud too much is in the title of his book. The name *Existential Psychoanalysis* suggests that Sartre will offer an alternative form of psychoanalysis. This he neither does nor seeks to do; indeed, he rightly acknowledges that a genuine existential psychoanalysis cannot yet be formulated or written. His book, rather, makes basic criticisms of modern psychology in general and of Freud's determinism in particular, and gives Sartre's often brilliant analysis of these errors and his proposals for their correction. He indicates also in what direction an existential psychoanalysis might be developed. Sartre does all of this on the basis of his existential understanding of man and his unshakable conviction that the human being simply cannot be understood at all if we see in him only what our study of subhuman forms of life permits us to see, or if we reduce him to naturalistic or mechanical determinisms, or fragmentize him into separate instincts or sets of stimuli and response, or in any other way take away from the man we try to study his ultimate freedom and individual responsibility.

Let me now mention some of the central and, in my judgment, highly significant points Sartre develops in *Existential Psychoanalysis*. I shall not try to do this logically or systematically, but rather in a way which I hope will indicate something of the nature and meaning of Sartre's contribution.

First Sartre points out that the usual forms of "explaining" which dominate most psychology and psychoanalysis simply do not explain at all. Using the case of Flaubert and the question of how he became a writer, Sartre points out that Bourget's "explanation" in terms of general emotional patterns and Flaubert's alleged need to escape into the less violent forms of expression in writing, covers up the very thing we need to understand. Also "explanations" estrange us from the person. We lose Flaubert.

The Freudian mechanisms like "projection," "introjection," "transference" do not explain either, since you never can leap from a general abstract law to a unique particular person. As many of us discover in psychoanalysis, the critical problem is always to know whether the general law can be *applied* to this particular person at this given moment in his history. This is the Achilles heel of all general laws used to explain individual human beings and is often blithely skipped over in our too simplified and too hasty beliefs in our special approach to science.

Nor will Sartre accept any "explanation" in terms of determinism by the past. Sartre is much too intelligent not to know that we are all subject to determining influences at every point. We are determined by our birth into a particular family of particular cultural and economic status, determined by our bodies, by instinctual needs, by past emotional traumas, and so on *ad infinitum*. The only trouble is, he argues, none of these explanations ever tells us what we want to know—why a given person like Flaubert at a given point in his history chooses to become a writer. And why does he affirm this decision in a hundred and one different ways and degrees at a hundred and one different times? The human reality, Sartre insists, "identifies and defines itself by the ends which it pursues," [5] not by alleged hypothetical "causes" in the past.

Nor can you explain the "higher" by the "lower" in evolutionary terms. The crucial problem in understanding man is not what attributes the human being shares with the horse or dog or rat, but what constitutes him uniquely as man.

Further, we cannot explain the person by recourse to talk about environment. Sartre insists, and I think very rightly, that "the environment can act on the subject only to the exact extent that he comprehends it; that he transforms it into a situation." [6] I take it that Sartre means by "comprehend" that the individual has a meaningful relationship with this "environment," this present situation. Many of us would (as Sartre would not) include elements of which the individual is unconscious in this meaningful relationship.

The psychoanalyst, Sartre goes on, will not be able to apply one-to-one specific symbols, but will have "to rediscover at each step a symbol functioning in the particular case which he is considering." Sartre feels that the splitting up of the person into ego and id does not help us. A person *is* his id only as he adopts a passive attitude toward it, that is, toward the so-called unconscious forces, urges, and so on, which Freud posited therein.

In all these emphases Sartre ranges himself, like the other phenomenological psychologists, firmly on the side of the "understanding" psychologies rather than the "explanatory" ones. Neverthless, existential psychology is not at all an anarchy or a form of mysticism, but will have its principles and its structure.

Now to the positive side of Sartre's psychoanalysis. The central principle of existential psychoanalysis will not be *libido* or *will to power,* but the individual's choice of being. "The goal of existential psychoanalysis is to rediscover through these empirical, concrete projects the original mode in which each man has chosen his being." [7] Again, "existential psychoanalysis is a method destined to bring to light, in a strictly objective form, the subjective choice by which each living person makes himself a person." [8] If we admit that the person is a totality, Sartre argues, we obviously cannot arrive at that totality by simply adding up diverse sums. We find it rather in a "choice of an intelligible character," for I am "nothing other than the choice of myself as a totality" [9] in a concrete relationship with the world.

Behind all this, of course, lies Sartre's insistence on individual responsibility: "I *am* my choices." The reader will understand this better if he thinks of choices not simply as the "big" resolutions made at New Year's but as the specific, intentional way I relate to my world at this given moment. Indeed, even free association in psychoanalysis, if it is to be fruitful and viable, depends upon this giving of one's self to the process, this taking a chance; even recalling a repressed childhood memory requires such an intentional orientation to the world of which memory is a part. I think Sartre oversimplifies the problem of freedom, as I said above. But I do not think we can avoid the searching cogency of his penetrating question, *Is not this choice the point par excellence in which we find revealed the totality of the human being?* As Paul Tillich remarks in another context, "Man becomes truly human only at the moment of decision."

Nor is this choice to be thought of as only on the level of consciousness, or consisting only of reflective, voluntary decisions. Sartre speaks of "spontaneous determinations of our being," and certainly he believes that in every choice the totality of the self—dreams, desires, tastes, powers, past experience, and future hopes—is involved. Thus in his concept of choice he seems to include some aspects of what the Freudians call the "unconscious."

The reader of Sartre will also be struck by his penetrating discussion of "bad faith." Bad faith means self-deceit. The human being is distinguished by the fact that he can lie to himself. And to do this remarkable thing requires that I know on some level that *I* am the one lying to myself; otherwise I couldn't to it. "The lie is a behavior of transcendence," Sartre well remarks.[10] To be in bad faith means to be guilty of not accepting one's self as a free person but taking it as an object. Sartre holds that classical psychoanalysis takes away just this crucial center of responsibility for one's own self-deceit; classical psychoanalysis, he charges, is based on the idea of a "lie without a liar."[11]

Sartre is constrained to deny the existence of "the unconscious," since even in self-deceit I know I am the one deceiving myself; and the so-called "censor" which Freud postulated as standing at the door of the unconscious must also be conscious in order to know what to repress. In his denial of "the unconscious" Sartre is in the general line of the phenomenological psychologists and psychiatrists such as Goldstein, Binswanger, and Boss.

So far as Sartre is attacking the "blank check" or "cellar" idea of the unconscious—the idea that we can explain anything by hypothesizing something down in the "unconscious"—I go along with him. But I believe he goes too far in his rejection.

Finally, we should note Sartre's emphasis on *ontology*—the study of being, what constitutes man as man—as the necessary basis for psychoanalysis. Where ontology stops, psychoanalysis begins; the "final discoveries of ontology are the first principles of psycho- analysis." [12] Ontology is a difficult concept, but given right definition, I believe Sartre's main idea here is entirely correct and very im- portant.

We repeat Sartre's caution at the close of one of his chapters: his "Psychoanalysis" is not supposed to be a newly worked-out technical system. He stated, as we have already said, that he did not believe that an existential psychoanalysis could yet be written; but he submits that the beginnings of it are present in various human docu- ments. Sartre himself believes in the great value of biographies, for example, for working out these principles. Like Allport, Maslow, McKinnon, and Murray among the psychologists in this country, Sartre would study the "successfully adjusted actions of life," the writer's style, and other constructive creative aspects of behavior. These reveal—if we can understand them—the central meaning of human experience as much as, and in some ways more than, neurosis and psychosis.

NOTES FOR CHAPTER 9

1. Miss Barnes is the translator of Sartre's larger book, *Being and Nothingness,* of which *Existential Psychoanalysis* is a part. The chapters on Sartre's psychology, entitled "A Psychology of Freedom," in Hazel Barnes' *The Literature of Possibility,* University of Ne- braska Press, Lincoln, 1959, are to be recommended.
2. Jean-Paul Sartre, *Existential Psychology,* Chicago, Regnéry, 1953, p. 44.
3. Jean-Paul Sartre, *Being and Nothingness,* translated by Hazel Barnes, New York, Philosophical Library, 1956, p. 561.
4. Paul Tillich, "Existentialism and Psychotherapy," *Review of Exis- tential Psychology and Psychiatry,* Vol. 1, No. 1, p. 9.
5. Sartre, *Existential Psychoanalysis,* p. 41.
6. *Ibid.,* p. 83.
7. *Ibid.,* p. 155.
8. *Ibid.,* p. 37.
9. *Ibid.,* p. 59.
10. *Ibid.,* p. 207.
11. *Ibid.,* p. 215.
12. *Ibid.,* p. 91.

10

Dangers in the Relation of Existentialism to Psychotherapy

> *And the tragic history of human thought is simply the history of a struggle between reason and life—reason bent on rationalizing life and forcing it to submit to the inevitable, to mortality; life bent on vitalizing reason and forcing it to serve as a support for its own vital desires.*
>
> —MIGUEL DE UNAMUNO, The Tragic Sense of Life

There has not yet been time for the existential approach in psychiatry and psychology to find its particular form in this country. Until recently, the writings and speeches on existential psychotherapy in America seemed to be a tower of Babel, a confusion of tongues. There were voices which said that existential psychology was Adlerian, others that it was all in Jung, others that it was encompassed in Freud, still others that it was identical with psychodrama, and so on. Existential psychiatry was identified with Zen Buddhism and anti-intellectual trends on one hand; or with a superintellectual philosophy composed of untranslatable German terms on the other. It was said to be therapy which everyone does when he is doing good therapy, and also to be—especially in its classical phenomenological wing—a philosophical analysis which had nothing to do with the practice of therapy as such. These spokesmen seemed blithely unaware of their patent contradictions: if existential psychotherapy is one of these things, it cannot be the others.

In the tower of Babel story in the book of Genesis, it will be recalled, the Lord sent the confusion to confound the pride and

147

grandiosity of the builders. I suspect that another purpose, or at least opportunity, which this confusion of voices lays upon us in our day is to force us to cut through the faddist and bandwagon tendencies which bedevil any new movement of ideas and to ask ourselves as incisively as possible what are the negative as well as the positive aspects of the present relation of existentialism to psychotherapy.

Since I have elsewhere concentrated on the positive aspects, I shall here cite some of the negative trends in this relationship.

A first trend that, in my judgment, is unconstructive is the anti-scientific tendency in some existential psychiatry and psychology. This trend has become linked with the anti-intellectual trend in our country. Certainly one of the abuses to which the existential movement in parts of Europe fell unhappy heir was the anti-intellectual tendency. But one cannot be against science or reason as such. I am reminded of Margaret Fuller's pompous statement, "I accept the universe," and Carlyle's rightfully famous rejoinder, "Gad, she'd better." For science is part of our universe, and it makes no sense not to accept it. The fact that many thoughtful psychiatrists and psychologists and other sensitive intelligent people in our culture recognize the inadequacies of present scientific method for a study of man should lead us not into an antiscientific trend but into the effort to find *new scientific methods which will be more adequate for revealing the nature of man.* The endeavors of our European colleagues, such as Binswanger, Buytendijk, and van den Berg to develop a phenomenological context for a science of man is in the constructive direction.

The same with anti-intellectualism. The tendency to distrust reason as such in our culture has arisen from the fact that the alternatives that intelligent and sensitive people have presented to them have seemed to be only arid rationalism and positivism on the one hand, in which one saves one's mind by losing one's soul, or vitalistic romanticism on the other, in which there has seemed at least a chance, for the time being, of saving one's soul.

The existentialists—from Kierkegaard, Nietzsche, and Schopenhauer down to the modern psychotherapists—are in a sense constructive anti-intellectualists. They stand against the compartmentalized rationalistic trend in nineteenth and twentieth century thought in the West. I do not mean in the slightest to compare them with the McCarthys, witch-hunters, and other political anti-intellectuals who endeavor to foment the anxiety of our time into hostility and hatred for purposes of their own power. The McCarthys bear the same relation to the thinkers I am talking about as Hitler's National Socialism did to true socialism, or that fascist collectivism does to cooperative economic and political community, or that any neurotic symptom does to a genuine need. But when destructive, neurotic developments occur in a society as in a person, it is almost always because some genuine and desperate need exists as an underlying cause.

It will help here to see the difference between intellectualization—which the existentialists revolt against—and anti-intellectualism. That we intellectuals tend to play into the compartmentalizing tendencies in our day can be demonstrated every day in psychotherapeutic work with intellectuals. Intellectuals as patients often use ideas as a substitute for experience and actual living. To talk about problems—and they are generally very good talkers—is frequently their defense against the anxiety which the problem engenders. They often operate on the assumption that if a problem can be formulated, something is changed; whereas in reality nothing at all may have occurred except the bolstering of a false sense of security based on the illusion that an idea has reality in itself. True, formulation does often help a person see his problem more clearly. But it can never be a substitute for pondering, feeling, experiencing the problem. True, also, genuine understanding does involve some change in the person. Socrates was not naive when he said that knowledge *is* virtue; but he meant knowledge which goes deep into the person's emotions, involving both rational and irrational experience, so-called "unconscious" material, ethical decision, and so forth. On the cultural level this kind of knowledge is also not merely intellectualistic but involves mythology, religious beliefs, and economic and political convictions.

It may well be true that if we can formulate a problem in inanimate nature thoroughly—that is, mathematically—we at the same time arrive at the solution; the formulation and the solution may be identical. But this is not true with people; here personal involvement, participation, and commitment are always necessary if the particular truth is to be real to that person. I think the chief reason many psychoanalyses of intellectuals have not been successful is that their problems tend to be intellectualized, and pseudo-scientific detachment takes the place of emotional involvement.

In psychotherapy, we have tended to commit the error of placing too much weight on verbalization. Verbalization, like formulation in the psychotherapeutic session, is useful only so long as it is an integral part of experiencing. People in therapy often talk because they are afraid of silence or afraid of directly experiencing themselves and the other person, the therapist. Indeed, when a person gets an insight, he may talk at length and with enthusiasm about it in order precisely to dilute it and thus avoid the full force of its consequence.

These points are of special importance because in our day in psychotherapy we tend to get relatively few of the hysterical types of patients Freud wrote about, who brought plenty of repressed emotion into the consulting room. We get more and more, rather, of the schizoid, unrelated types who have learned to cover up their loneliness and isolation by talking with great facility *about* relationships, and who experience according to rules and plans rather than directly. Many of these persons who get to our clinics are not intellectuals in any professional or serious sense, but they have read about psychotherapy and Oedipus complexes and whatnot, and they are often already adept at discussing their problems at great length. It seems that everyone in our schizoid age is trying to be an intellectual in the bad sense; that is, trying to live out his life by talking, and he believes he is successful if he makes the talk scientifically and rationally respectable.

The danger that the existential approach in psychology and psychiatry may play into the hands of detachment and intellectualizing is particularly seductive because the use of existential terms lends a semblance of dealing with human reality when one may not be doing so at all. Many of us have criticized orthodox psychoanalysis because its technique can be used as a convenient screen behind which the therapist can hide in the so-called "impersonal mirror," avoiding full encounter, full presence in the relation with the other person. Such encounter has the power to shake us deeply and is anxiety-creating as well as joy-creating. Hence therapists must be aware of all tendencies to avoid it, including the tendency to be philosophically as well as technically detached.

Now the existential approach is not to be rationalistic or anti-rationalistic, *but to seek the underlying ground in human experience in which both reason and unreason are based.* We must not be "mis-ologists," Socrates cautions us; but the "logos" must be made flesh.

The essay by Paul Tillich, "Existentialism and Psychotherapy," [1] is a splendid example of the profound union of reason with the existential inquiry that goes beyond mere rationalism. Tillich is existential without rejecting essences and logical structure. The scholarly work of R. D. Laing also seems to me to show this endeavor.

THE SECOND negative trend is the tendency to identify existential psychiatry with Zen Buddhism. The widespread interest in Zen, especially among intellectuals in this country, has been a symptom of the constructive religious questioning of our day. Let me state immediately that I have great respect for Zen Buddhism as represented by those genuinely devoted to it, like Suzuki. I also value the serious interpretations of it by Western writers, despite my disagreement with some of their points. Zen Buddhism has genuine importance as a corrective to our Western overactivism; its emphases on immediacy of experience, *being* rather than mere *doing,* are a great relief and offer significant guidance to many sorely beset competitive and driven Westerners.

But the identification of Zen Buddhism with existential psychiatry is a different matter. It oversimplifies both. One of my colleagues, doing research in a mental hospital, holds that he has repeatedly achieved satori by means of the drug lysergic acid. Then "working back from the drug experience," he writes, "I have finally reached satori repeatedly without the drug." Now satori is the result of years of discipline. If we can achieve it so easily by drugs, why do we need Zen Buddhism or any other religion? And if we can overcome the despair, the agony, the *angst* of life that way, we certainly shall not need any psychotherapy. As William Barrett asked in his review of a book by Alan Watts in the *New York Times,* referring to Watts's similar claim of achieving satori by means of the drug, on which criteria are what authorities going to decide who receives the drug and who does not?

The liaison between oversimplified Zen Buddhism and existential psychiatry has within it, as I have observed it, the tendency to bypass and evade anxiety, tragedy, guilt, and the reality of evil. One of the lasting contributions of the psychotherapeutic movement in all its forms has been in helping people frankly to admit and confront their *angst,* hostility, and guilt, to face the fact of destructiveness and evil psychologically as well as culturally in the world. The existential approach is the achieving of individuality not by avoiding the conflictual realities of the world in which we find ourselves (which for us is perforce Western culture), but by confronting these directly, and through the meeting of them to achieve individuality and meaningful interpersonal relations.

It is important to make these criticisms in order that the positive contribution of Eastern thought to our Western parochialism may not be lost. Zen Buddhism has had and will continue to have (if its adherents do not run it into the ground) radical significance as a corrective to Western overindividualized will and consciousness.

A final word about LSD and the other hallucinogenic drugs. It is difficult to have a balanced perception of this topic in the contemporary phobic and counterphobic atmosphere. Those who have taken the drug tend to speak of it as a religious experience and are irrationally "pro," whereas those who are against use of the drugs—and they include a good part of the officialdom in this country at the moment—are irrationally afraid of threats to their own rationality. I shall make some comments about the drugs on the basis of the extensive research being conducted at the William Alanson White Institute—the professional group with which I am connected—into the use of LSD in psychotherapy.

There seems to be no doubt but that, by and large, the researching therapists believe LSD is useful in therapy. (They give a much smaller dose than that taken for the purpose of a religious, mystical experience.) The patients when given the drug seem to be characterized by greater emotionality, decrease in defensiveness, loosening of associations, and capacity to be taken up by the immediate situation and to become intensively preoccupied with themselves. Most people who take it seem to report a positive experience, ranging from euphoria to ecstasy. But persons who have a tendency toward disorganization may become definitely disorganized and go into a painful psychotic state. The term "mind-expanding" is a misnomer for the drug. In Europe, where it has been used a longer time, it is called "mind-dissolving" rather than "mind-expanding" (psycholytic rather than psychedelic) and the former term is more accurate. For the drug itself puts nothing inside you: it simply makes it possible, through breaking down certain mental functions, to experience one's self and world with telescopic intensity. The person's field of vision is magnified and concentrated, and he may feel himself in touch with primeval and original experience which assumedly antedates the subject-object dichotomy. But it is neither desirable nor possible to live permanently on such a level. Promiscuous and dilettante taking of the drug seems often to dull the person's relation to reality and result in a naive, grossly oversimplified attitude to life. The real question is, what new structure of himself does the person build?

My colleagues who work intensively in this field report that there is no evidence that taking LSD increases the creative capacities of *creative* persons.[2] It may sufficiently shock noncreative people that they find some creative possibilities in their lives. But the value or lack of value of taking the drug lies in the preparation for and the working through of the experience afterwards. Persons who have had a good deal of analysis but are up against roadblocks, and persons who have had religious discipline, seem most helped. I propose a positive attitude toward the possibilities of such drugs. But by the same token I propose that the "religious faith" that this or any drug will be the panacea that elevates us into a brave new world free from the human dilemma is a naive and misleading illusion. In the devotion to the drugs I hear an anguished cry against our schizoid, depersonalized society, "We need something—anything—to enable us to feel *personal* again!" [3]

A THIRD DANGER in existential psychiatry and psychology arises directly out of the above. It is the tendency to use such terms as "transcendence," "encounter," "presence" as a way of bypassing existential reality. We hear in discussions and papers, for example, such references to the "transcendence" assumedly occurring in psychotherapy as "transcendence of the subject-object dichotomy between therapist and patient," "transcendence of the body-mind dichotomy," "transcendence of dualistic thought," "transcendence of the epistemic barrier between man and Ultimate Reality [God]." The term "encounter" is used—or rather misused—with a kind of halo to varnish over the very difficult problems of interpersonal relationships and their distortion, and the term "presence" is misused to cover up the fact that understanding another person genuinely is a very difficult process in the best of situations and is never possible in a complete sense.

What happens in such an approach is that practically all the age-old problems of human existence, with which thinkers have struggled since human consciousness was born, are bypassed by a word. It has been argued that in the "transcendence of dualistic thought," for example, the therapist uses a mode of thinking that is "beyond language and symbolic imagery," that he is freed from concepts which hamper "the capacity to see what really is," and that in such "moments of understanding there is no understander."

But symbols, language of one form or another, are always the form and content of any thinking. Is it not manifestly impossible to use a mode of thought that goes beyond symbolic imagery? Husserl's phenomenological approach is often mistakenly applied to mean that the psychotherapist observes a patient without any concepts presupposed in the therapist's mind at all. But this too is impossible. Concepts are the orientation by which perception occurs. Without some concepts presupposed the therapist would not see the patient who is there or anything about him.

Certainly there must be an "understander" if there is to be understanding. I am quite aware of the arguments, often having their base in Buddhistic and other Eastern religions that in moments of deep understanding it is "as though" the two persons were completely merged. But this is a religious dimension, and it only confuses both science and religion to make it identical with psychotherapy. The subjective experience of being "merged" which does occur rightfully between therapist and patient is one of instantaneous alternation with the objective pole, namely, the awareness on the part of the therapist that he indeed is the therapist, not the patient, and that he will genuinely help the patient to the extent that he in his own integrity does not give up his identity.

There is another value, therapeutic and moral, in keeping clear the distinction between the two persons. For if the therapist realizes that he is always seeing the patient through his own eyes, understanding the patient in his own way no matter how wise or well-analyzed or broad-minded he is, he will be aware that his understanding will always be limited and biased to some extent. This makes for a humility, a quality of mercy and forgiveness in human relations which is highly therapeutic. If the therapist does not assume this but absolutizes his own perception and understanding, he will automatically dominate the patient by his own subjectivity, a danger against which Sartre has warned us. Then the therapist is playing God as surely as if he had an absolute technique. The existential therapist can overcome so far as possible his own tendency to strait-jacket the patient by subjectivity by admitting his own bias and limitations to start with. Once these are admitted, the phenomenological approach can be of great help, as many of us have discovered, in seeing and relating to the patient as he really is.

A final danger is making existential psychiatry into a special school. There are serious errors, in my judgment, in such an approach. One is that there cannot be any special "existential psychiatry," as Leslie Farber has well remarked, any more than there can be Hegelian, Platonic, or Spinozist psychiatry. Existentialism is an *attitude,* an approach to human beings, rather than a special school or group. Like any philosophy, it has to do with the *presuppositions* underlying psychiatric and psychoanalytic technique.

It is doubtful, for example, whether it makes any sense to speak of an "existential psychotherapist" in a technical sense at this stage of the development of the movement. The existential approach is not a system of therapy—though it makes highly important contributions to therapy. It is not a set of techniques—though it may give birth to them. It is rather a concern with understanding the structure of the human being and his experience which to a greater or lesser extent should underlie *all* technique. Many of those who call themselves existential psychoanalysts already presuppose a long and complex training in psychoanalysis or some other form of therapy.[4]

I obviously do not imply that the existential approach must be allied with the particular form of psychotherapy called psychoanalysis. Nor do I deny that attitudes and presuppositions about human beings will be more determinant (as Rogers' studies have shown) of the success of psychotherapy than the particular technical school to which the therapist belongs. But we must not fall into the frequently oversimplified sentimental view that implies that in psychotherapy mere benevolence is enough.

There is another emphasis which, to my mind, is in error—the "psychological analysis of being." Now you cannot analyze being, and if you could do so it would be a harmful thing to do. *Being* must be assumed in psychotherapy, not analyzed. An individual's being is shown, for example, in his right to exist as a person, his possibilities for self-respect and his ultimate freedom to choose his own way of life. All these must be assumed when we work with a patient, and if we cannot assume them about a given person, we should not work with that patient. To try to analyze these evidences of being is to violate the fundamental being of the person himself. Bringing our technical attitudes to bear on being itself is to repeat the same error for which existentialists justly criticize not only classical psychoanalysis but our whole culture, i.e., making the person subordinate to techniques. To analyze the "psyche" as in psychoanalysis is difficult enough and can and should be done only within limits. The blockages the person suffers which will not let him gain adequate self-esteem, for example, can be analyzed. But that is a far different thing from analyzing ontology, calling into question the fundamental qualities which constitute the person as a human being. To analyze being is parallel to repressing it in the sense that it subordinates being to a technical attitude; except that analyzing is a little more harmful in that it gives the therapist a nice rationalization for his repression and relieves him of guilt for his failure to exhibit the reverence and humility with which being should rightly be regarded.

Another way of putting our criticism of the "psychological analysis of being" emphasis is that psychoanalysis begins at the point where ontology leaves off. As Sartre well puts it, "The final discoveries of ontology are the first principles of psychoanalysis." [5]

Having cited these criticisms, I end by saying that I believe the movement in modern thought called existentialism will make a unique and highly significant contribution to the future of psychotherapy.

NOTES FOR CHAPTER 10

1. Paul Tillich, "Existentialism and Psychotherapy," *Review of Existential Psychology and Psychiatry,* Vol. 1, No. 1, 1961.
2. It seems fairly well agreed that Aldous Huxley's *Brave New World,* for example, is a great book, and that the companion piece to it, a novel written after Huxley had become interested in the drugs, *Island,* is like most of Huxley's productions during those later years, simply not much good as a novel. How much we can relate his literary productions to his taking of the drug is of course an open question.
3. We can empathize with this anguished cry without overlooking the irony of the situation, that the cry for the drugs makes the same mistake as technology, namely, expecting something introduced from *outside* the individual to save him.
4. My own training is in the William Alanson White Psychoanalytic Institute. I identify myself as a psychoanalyst of this approach—which does not make me any the less existential in my presuppositions.
5. Jean-Paul Sartre, *Existential Psychoanalysis,* 1953, p. 91.

Part Four

Freedom and Responsibility

There is agreement among many psychotherapists that the enlarging of the individual's responsible freedom is one of the goals, if not the central goal of therapy. We shall also propose here that the enlarging of such responsible freedom is essential to the constructive confronting of the inescapable dilemmas of being human.

11

The Man Who Was Put in a Cage

> *What a piece of work is man! how noble in reason!*
> *how infinite in faculty! in form and moving how ex-*
> *press and admirable! . . . The paragon of animals!*
> —SHAKESPEARE, Hamlet

We have quite a few discrete pieces of information these days about what happens to a person when he is deprived of this or that element of freedom. We have our studies of sensory deprivation and of how a person reacts when put in different kinds of authoritarian atmosphere, and so on. But recently I have been wondering what pattern would emerge if we put these various pieces of knowledge together. In short, what would happen to a living, whole person if his total freedom—or as nearly total as we can imagine—were taken away? In the course of these reflections, a parable took form in my mind.

THE STORY BEGINS with a king who, while standing in reverie at the window of his palace one evening, happened to notice a man in the town square below. He was apparently an average man, walking home at night, who had taken the same route five nights a week for many years. The king followed this man in his imagination—pictured him arriving home, perfunctorily kissing his wife, eating his late meal, inquiring whether everything was all right with the children, reading the paper, going to bed, perhaps engaging in the sex relation with his wife or perhaps not, sleeping, and getting up and going off to work again the next day.

161

And a sudden curiosity seized the king, which for a moment banished his fatigue: "I wonder what would happen if a man were kept in a cage, like the animals at the zoo?" His curiosity was perhaps in some ways not unlike that of the first surgeons who wondered what it would be like to perform a lobotomy on the human brain.

So the next day the king called in a psychologist, told him of his idea, and invited him to observe the experiment. When the psychologist demurred saying, "It's an unthinkable thing to keep a man in a cage," the monarch replied that many rulers had in effect, if not literally, done so, from the time of the Romans through Genghis Khan down to Hitler and the totalitarian leaders; so why not find out scientifically what would happen? Furthermore, added the king, he had made up his mind to do it whether the psychologist took part or not; he had already gotten the Greater Social Research Foundation to give a large sum of money for the experiment, and why let that money go to waste? By this time the psychologist also was feeling within himself a great curiosity about what would happen if a man were kept in a cage.

And so the next day the king caused a cage to be brought from the zoo—a large cage that had been occupied by a lion when it was new, then later by a tiger; just recently it had been the home of a hyena who died the previous week. The cage was put in an inner private court in the palace grounds, and the average man whom the king had seen from the window was brought and placed therein. The psychologist, with his Rorschach and Wechsler-Bellevue tests in his brief case to administer at some appropriate moment, sat down outside the cage.

At first the man was simply bewildered, and he kept saying to the psychologist, "I have to catch the tram, I have to get to work, look what time it is, I'll be late for work!" But later on in the afternoon the man began soberly to realize what was up, and then he protested vehemently, "The king can't do this to me! It is unjust! It's against the law." His voice was strong, and his eyes full of anger. The psychologist liked the man for his anger, and he became vaguely aware that this was a mood he had encountered often in people he worked with in his clinic. "Yes," he realized, "this anger is the attitude of people who—like the healthy adolescents of any era—want to fight what's wrong, who protest directly against it. When people come to the clinic in this mood, it is good—they can be helped."

During the rest of the week the man continued his vehement protests. When the king walked by the cage, as he did every day, the man made his protests directly to the monarch.

But the king answered, "Look here, you are getting plenty of food, you have a good bed, and you don't have to work. We take good care of you; so why are you objecting?"

After some days has passed, the man's protests lessened and then ceased. He was silent in his cage, generally refusing to talk. But the psychologist could see hatred glowing in his eyes. When he did exchange a few words, they were short, definite words uttered in the strong, vibrant, but calm voice of the person who hates and knows whom he hates.

Whenever the king walked into the courtyard, there was a deep fire in the man's eyes. The psychologist thought, "This must be the way people act when they are first conquered." He remembered that he had also seen that expression of the eyes and heard that tone of voice in many patients at his clinic: the adolescent who had been unjustly accused at home or in school and could do nothing about it; the college student who was required by public and campus opinion to be a star on the gridiron, but was required by his professors to pass courses he could not prepare for if he were to be successful in football—and who was then expelled from college for the cheating that resulted. And the psychologist, looking at the active hatred in the man's eyes, thought, "It is still good; a person who has this fight in him can be helped."

Every day the king, as he walked through the courtyard, kept reminding the man in the cage that he was given food and shelter and taken good care of, so why did he not like it? And the psychologist noticed that, whereas at first the man had been entirely impervious to the king's statements, it now seemed more and more that he was pausing for a moment after the king's speech—for a second the hatred was postponed from returning to his eyes—as though he were asking himself if what the king said were possibly true.

And after a few weeks more, the man began to discuss with the psychologist how it was a useful thing that a man is given food and shelter; and how man had to live by his fate in any case, and the part of wisdom was to accept fate. He soon was developing an extensive theory about security and the acceptance of fate, which sounded to the psychologist very much like the philosophical theories that Rosenberg and others worked out for the fascists in Germany. He was very voluble during this period, talking at length, although the talk was mostly a monologue. The psychologist noticed that his voice was flat and hollow as he talked, like the voice of people in TV previews who make an effort to look you in the eye and try hard to sound sincere as they tell you that you should see the program they are advertising, or the announcers on the radio who are paid to persuade you that you should like highbrow music.

And the psychologist also noticed that now the corners of the man's mouth always turned down, as though he were in some gigantic pout. Then the psychologist suddenly remembered: this was like the middle-aged, middle-class people who came to his clinic, the respectable bourgeois people who went to church and lived morally but who were always full of resentment, as though everything they did was conceived, born, and nursed in resentment. It reminded the psychologist of Nietzsche's saying that the middle class was consumed with resentment. He then for the first time began to be seriously worried about the man in the cage, for he knew that once resentment gets a firm start and becomes well rationalized and structuralized, it may become like cancer. When the person no longer knows whom he hates, he is much harder to help.

During this period the Greater Social Research Foundation had a board of trustees meeting, and they decided that since they were expending a fund to keep a man supported in a cage, it would look better if representatives of the Foundation at least visited the experiment. So a group of people, consisting of two professors and a few graduate students, came in one day to look at the man in the cage.

One of the professors then proceeded to lecture to the group about the relation of the autonomic nervous system and the secretions of the ductless glands to human existence in a cage. But it occurred to the other professor that the verbal communications of the victim himself might just possibly be interesting, so he asked the man how he felt about living in a cage. The man was friendly toward the professors and students and explained to them that he had chosen this way of life, that there were great values in security and in being taken care of, that they would of course see how sensible his course was, and so on.

"How strange!" thought the psychologist, "and how pathetic; why is it he struggles so hard to get them to approve his way of life?"

In the succeeding days when the king walked through the courtyard, the man fawned upon him from behind the bars in his cage and thanked him for the food and shelter. But when the king was not in the yard and the man was not aware that the psychologist was present, his expression was quite different—sullen and morose. When his food was handed to him through the bars by the keeper, the man would often drop the dishes or dump over the water and then would be embarrassed because of his stupidity and clumsiness. His conversation became increasingly one-tracked; and instead of the involved philosophical theories about the value of being taken care of, he had gotten down to simple sentences such as "It is fate," which he would say over and over again, or he would just mumble to himself, "It is." The psychologist was surprised to find that the man should now be so clumsy as to drop his food, or so stupid as to talk in those barren sentences, for he knew from his tests that the man had originally been of good average intelligence. Then it dawned upon the psychologist that this was the kind of behavior he had observed in some anthropological studies among the Negroes in the South—people who had been forced to kiss the hand that fed and enslaved them, who could no longer either hate or rebel. The man in the cage took more and more to simply sitting all day long in the sun as it came through the bars, his only movement being to shift his position from time to time from morning through the afternoon.

It was hard to say just when the last phase set in. But the psychologist became aware that the man's face now seemed to have no particular expression; his smile was no longer fawning, but simply empty and meaningless, like the grimace a baby makes when there is gas on its stomach. The man ate his food and exchanged a few sentences with the psychologist from time to time; but his eyes were distant and vague, and though he looked at the psychologist, it seemed that he never really *saw* him.

And now the man, in his desultory conversations, never used the word "I" any more. He had accepted the cage. He had no anger, no hate, no rationalizations. But he was now insane.

The night the psychologist realized this, he sat in his apartment trying to write a concluding report. But it was very difficult for him to summon up words, for he felt within himself a great emptiness. He kept trying to reassure himself with the words, "They say that nothing is ever lost, that matter is merely changed to energy and back again." But he could not help feeling that something *had* been lost, that something had gone out of the universe in this experiment.

He finally went to bed with his report unfinished. But he could not sleep; there was a gnawing within him which, in less rational and scientific ages, would have been called a conscience. Why didn't I tell the king that this is the one experiment that no man can do— or at least why didn't I shout that I would have nothing to do with the whole bloody business? Of course, the king would have dismissed me, the foundations would never have granted me any more money, and at the clinic they would have said that I was not a real scientist. But maybe one could farm in the mountains and make a living, and maybe one could paint or write something that would make future men happier and more free. . . .

But he realized that these musings were, at least at the moment, unrealistic, and he tried to pull himself back to reality. All he could get, however, was this feeling of emptiness within himself, and the words, "Something has been taken out of the universe, and there is left only a void."

Finally he dropped off to sleep. Some time later, in the small hours of the morning, he was awakened by a startling dream. A crowd of people had gathered, in the dream, in front of the cage in the courtyard, and the man in the cage—no longer inert and vacuous—was shouting through the bars of the cage in impassioned oratory. "It is not only I whose freedom is taken away!" he was crying. "When the king puts me or any man in a cage, the freedom of each one of you is taken away also. The king must go!" The people began to chant, "The king must go!" and they seized and broke out the iron bars of the cage, and wielded them for weapons as they charged the palace.

The psychologist awoke, filled by the dream with a great feeling of hope and joy—an experience of hope and joy probably not unlike that experienced by the free men of England when they forced King John to sign the Magna Charta. But not for nothing had the psychologist had an orthodox analysis in the course of his training, and as he lay surrounded by this aura of happiness, a voice spoke within him: "Aha, you had this dream to make yourself feel better; it's just a wish fulfillment."

"The hell it is!" said the psychologist as he climbed out of bed. "Maybe some dreams are to be acted on."

12

Freedom and Responsibility Reexamined

> *Yes! to this thought I hold with firm persistence;*
> *The last result of wisdom stamps it true;*
> *He only earns his freedom and existence*
> *Who daily conquers them anew.*
>
> —GOETHE, Faust

The problems of freedom and responsibility are fundamental in a number of ways in counseling and psychotherapy. But we find ourselves in recent years caught in several pressing and critical dilemmas with respect to these issues. The dilemmas are part and parcel of the radical shift and transition of values in the last three or four decades in Western culture, particularly in America. It is, of course, not at all an accident that these are also exactly the decades when counseling, psychotherapy, and psychoanalysis have come to play such important roles in our society. For it is precisely the breakdown and radical transition of values in a society, causing the individuals in that society to founder in storm-shaken seas without solid mooring posts or even buoys and lighthouses which can be depended upon, that makes the professions of helping individuals so necessary.

Several "solutions" have arisen to the dilemmas we face in freedom and responsibility. I wish to cite some of these solutions which I believe to be inadequate, and then turn to what I hope will be a deeper examination of the problems of freedom and responsibility.

One inadequate solution was the assumption, popular a decade or two ago, that our task in counseling and therapy was simply to set the person "free," and, therefore, the values held by the therapist and the society had no part in the process. This assumption was bolstered and rationalized by the then popular definition of mental health as "freedom from anxiety." The therapists most under the influence of this assumption made a dogma out of never making a "moral judgment" and saw guilt as always neurotic and therefore a "feeling" that ought always to be relieved and gotten rid of in counseling and therapy. I recall that in my student days in psychoanalysis in the early 1940's it was argued by competent and experienced analysts that whether or not the patient was a gangster or a responsible member of society was no business of theirs—their task was only to help him become free to do better whatever he wished.

Probably most therapists had enough common sense and simple humanity never to follow out such a naive assumption to its full implications. But the subtle effects of the "values-don't-matter" assumption were in my judgment harmful and are in part responsible for the later reactions against psychoanalysis and counseling. One harmful effect was the implication that sexuality was, as Kinsey phrased it, a matter of "release" on a "sexual object." The accent upon sexual promiscuity—which developed paradoxically enough into a new dogma that to be healthy you had to be completely permissive sexually—led to new anxiety and insecurity in the whole area of sexual behavior among our contemporaries. The plethora of early marriages we have been witnessing among college students in the past decade seems to me to be, at least in part, a reaction to the insecurity, anxiety, and loneliness involved in the doctrine of sexual promiscuity. For the "full freedom" assumption we are describing actually separates and alienates the person from his world, removes whatever structure he had to act within or against, and leaves him with no guideposts in a lonely, worldless existence.

The errors in the "full freedom" assumption were not only that it led to increase of anxiety among counselees and patients, but also that it was subtly dishonest. For no matter how much the therapist or counselor might protest that he assumed no values in his practice, the patient or counselee knew, even if he did not dare to express his knowledge, that the protestation was not true; and that the therapist was smuggling in his own values the more perniciously in the very fact of not admitting them.

Another "solution" offered to our dilemma arose in the last decade as a reaction to the one mentioned above. This is the *distrust of freedom* present so much in the psychological and psychiatric discussions around us these days. It is an overemphasis on "responsibility," but put in the form of moral and social control of the other person. The contemporary trends toward conformism and the tremendous pressures toward standardization which inevitably accompany television and mass communication give impetus to this tendency toward control. William H. Whyte in his *Organization Man* is quite accurate in his pithy cautions to psychologists and psychiatrists at these points. He succinctly states that modern man's enemies may turn out to be "mild looking groups of therapists who . . . would be doing what they did to help you." He refers to the inevitable tendency to use the social ethic of our particular historical period. And thus the very process of helping people may actually make them more conformist and destroy individuality.

Several other social critics have pointed out recently that we are witnessing the birth in psychiatry and psychology of a "new puritanism" and new emphasis on "behavior control." The new puritanism has until recently been most evident in psychiatry, but now emphases on moralism have come from psychologists in the therapeutic field. Whereas a plethora of books came off the psychiatric presses two decades ago adjuring you to "release your sexual tensions" and "express yourself fully," in the last five years the books tell us "Divorce Won't Help" and advise us that "monogamy is the new dogma of science." The new moralism among psychologists is illustrated by the works on therapy of Hobart Mowrer and of Perry London, and by what is termed "reality therapy." [1] As I shall indicate below, I believe that both the exaggerated freedom solution and the identification of therapy and counseling with the moral and social controls of the society are inadequate.

As the new puritanism is represented in psychiatry and psychotherapy, the new emphasis upon "control of the mind and personality," as a denial of the freedom of the person, is perhaps most present in academic psychology. This phase of the dilemma is graphically illustrated by an exchange between Carl Rogers and B. F. Skinner, which I wish to cite. In connection with the most extreme form of this in the operant conditioning of Skinner, Rogers writes:

> Along with the development of technology has gone an underlying philosophy of rigid determinism as illustrated by a brief exchange which I had with Professor B. F. Skinner of Harvard at a recent conference. A paper given by Dr. Skinner led me to direct these remarks to him. "From what I understood Dr. Skinner to say, it is his understanding that though he might have thought he chose to come to this meeting, might have thought he had a purpose in giving his speech, such thoughts are really illusory. He actually made certain marks on paper and emitted certain sounds here simply because his genetic make-up and his past environment had operantly conditioned his behavior in such a way that it was rewarding to make these sounds, and that he as a person doesn't enter into this. In fact if I get his thinking correctly, from his strictly scientific point of view, he, as a person, doesn't exist." In his reply Dr. Skinner said that he would not go into the question of whether he had any choice in the matter (presumably because the whole issue is illusory) but stated, "I do accept your characterization of my own presence here." I do not need to labor the point that for Dr. Skinner the concept of "learning to be free" would be quite meaningless.[2]

We could of course multiply our illustrations many times over to support the point that the issues of freedom and responsibility, choice and determinism, are central and critical in American psychology.

I WISH TO BEGIN my reexamination of freedom and responsibility by considering this present emphasis upon control. The phrases "control of behavior" and "control of the mind and personality," which I shall use somewhat synonymously in this discussion, raise disquieting questions. Control implies control *by* someone or something. *Who* would control the mind? The person himself? In that case some aspect of his mind or self would be doing the controlling. But this view is not acceptable, for we then find ourselves assuming a fragmented view of the self which is scarcely tenable and only makes our problem more confused. Or do we mean society controls the mind? But society is simply made up of us persons whose "minds" are assumedly to be controlled.

Does the phrase mean that some special group of us—psychiatrists, psychologists, or other scientists—will control the mind, meaning other people's minds? Unfortunately, I think this is the unscrutinized subconscious assumption of many people who use the phrase, namely, that their group will do the controlling, as though *we* knew how the minds of *others* should be controlled. Recently I participated in an emergency conference of psychiatrists and psychologists concerning the pressing problem of war and peace. Several of the papers at the conference proposed that psychiatrists and psychologists be sent to trouble spots in the world, interview diplomats around the globe and report back to their respective state departments their findings so that statesmen with paranoid tendencies and serious maladjustments will be recalled. The trouble with this plan is that such "diagnoses," if they may be called that, always presuppose some criteria and goals as the basis on which you judge. Fortunately, there seems to be no chance whatever that any state department would ever permit any group to arrogate to itself this kind of control. I say fortunately, because there is no reason to believe that the judgments with respect to the goals of life are any better among psychiatrists and psychologists as a group than among philosophers or statesmen themselves, or theologians, writers, or artists.

We note that the word "goals" has now crept into our discussion. It is impossible to keep it out. For control always implies not only control *by* something but *for* something. For what purposes, which means on the basis of which *values,* will the mind be controlled and toward what ends will this control be directed? This disconcerting question has in the past been generally sloughed over in psychological discussions with the rejoinder that as scientists we deal only with means, not goals. But is this not a highly dubious and possibly dangerous attitude? And is not this separation of means and ends even part of the reason for our predicament in twentieth-century civilization, namely, that we possess such powerful means of controlling nature and ourselves—drugs, atomic power, etc.—but we have not kept pace in analyzing what we are controlling for?

Or if we accept the proposal sometimes made in psychological conferences that our computers can set our goals, our technicians determine our policies, we are in my judgment making the most serious error of all. For we are abdicating in the face of our lack of goals and values. The one thing our computers cannot tell us is what our goals ought to be. In this day when we and all sensitive contemporary people are so confused and anxious, it is not surprising we tend to abdicate in favor of the machine. We then tend more and more to ask only the questions the machine can answer, we teach more and more only the things the machine can teach, and limit our research to the quantitative work the machines can do. There then is bound to emerge a real and inexorable tendency to make our image of man over into the image of the very machine by which we study and control him.

We must seek, I submit, a new and deeper understanding of freedom which will stand even in a world in which exist such vast and overwhelming pressures toward control. To do this we must begin, in my judgment, with the question of what are the distinguishing characteristics of this being, man, whom we are trying to understand.

A CENTRAL DISTINGUISHING characteristic, we have seen, is man's capacity to be aware of himself as having a world and being interrelated with it. Now weighing the long-term future consequences of his acts—which we have also seen as a capacity of man—is a *social* act and inevitably implies value-judgments. Hence the concepts of mind and personality imply the distinctively *social-historical* development which characterizes human beings. Man, as we indicated in a previous chapter, is not merely pushed blindly by the march of history, is not *just* the product of history (as all animals are), but he has the capacity to be self-aware of his history. He can exercise selectivity toward history, can adapt himself to parts of it, can change other parts, and within limits mold history in self-chosen directions. This capacity to transcend the immediate situation and bring the time determinant into learning gives human behavior its distinctive flexibility and freedom.

We find, lo and behold, that in defining mind and personality we have also been talking about *freedom*. For is not man's capacity to be conscious of himself as the experiencing individual actually also the psychological basis of human freedom? Hegel puts our point in one powerful sentence: "The history of the world is none other than the progress of the consciousness of freedom."

The data we get from our work with patients in psychotherapy seem to me clearly to support my thesis. When people come for therapy, they typically describe themselves as "driven," unable to know or choose what they want, and they experience various degrees of dissatisfaction, unhappiness, conflict, and despair. What we find as we begin working with them is that they have blocked off large areas of awareness, are unable to feel or be aware of what their feelings mean in relation to the world. They may think they feel love when actually they only feel sex; or they think they feel sex when what they actually wish is to be nursed at mother's breast. They will often say in one way or another: "I don't know what I feel; I don't know who I am." In Freud's terms, they have "repressed" significant experiences and capacities of all sorts. The symptomatic results are the wide gamut of conflicts, anxiety, panic, and depression.

At the beginning of therapy, thus, they present the picture of *lack* of freedom. The progress of therapy can be gauged in terms of the increase of the patient's capacity to experience the fact he is the one who *has* this world and can be aware of it and move in it.[3] One could define mental health, from one side, as the capacity to be aware of the gap between stimulus and response, together with the capacity to use this gap constructively. Thus, mental health, in my judgment, is on the opposite side of the spectrum from "conditioning" and "control." The progress of therapy can be measured in terms of the progress of "consciousness of freedom."

Self implies world, and world, self; each concept—or experience— requires the other. Now, contrary to the usual assumption, these vary upward and downward on the scale together: broadly speaking, the more awareness of self, the more awareness of world, and vice versa.

Patients on the verge of psychosis will often reveal overwhelming anxiety as the panic at losing awareness of themselves and their world simultaneously. To lose one's self is to lose one's world, and vice versa.

This inseparable relation of self and world also implies *responsibility*. The term means "responding," "response to." I cannot, in other words, become a self except as I am engaged continuously in *responding* to the world of which I am a part.

What is exceedingly interesting here is that the patient moves *toward* freedom and responsibility in his living as he becomes more conscious of the *deterministic* experiences in his life. That is, as he explores and assimilates how he was rejected or overprotected or hated as a child, how his repressed bodily needs drive him, how his personal history as a member of a minority group, let us say, conditions his development, and even as he becomes more conscious of his being a member of Western culture at a particular traumatic moment in the historical evolution of that society, he finds his margin of freedom likewise enlarged. As he becomes more conscious of the infinite deterministic forces in his life, he becomes more free.

The implications of this point are very significant. *Freedom* is thus not the opposite to determinism. Freedom is the individual's capacity *to know that he is the determined one,* to pause between stimulus and response and thus to throw his weight, however slight it may be, on the side of one particular response among several possible ones.

Freedom is thus also not anarchy: the beatniks are a symbolic protest against the aridity of our mechaniistic society, not an expression of freedom. Freedom can never be separated from responsibility.

Let us now turn to another source of data bearing on our problem. These data are dramatic and vivid but also very important—the experiences of individuals in imprisonment and concentration camps. One might well think that talking about "consciousness of freedom" in such places of terrible travesty on human dignity would be sheer sentimentality. But we find just the opposite may be the case.

Christopher Burney, a young British secret service officer, was dropped behind enemy lines during World War II and captured by the Germans. He was put in solitary confinement, without a book, pencil, or sheet of paper, for eighteen months. In his six-by-six cell, Burney decided that each day he would review in his mind lesson after lesson he had studied in school and college. He worked through theorems in geometry, the thought of Spinoza and other philosophers, outlined in his mind the literature he had read, and so on. In his book *Solitary Confinement* he demonstrates how this "freedom of the mind," as he called it, kept him sane for the eighteen solitary months and made his survival possible.

From the horrors of the Dachau concentration camp, Dr. Bruno Bettleheim reports that he learned a similar lesson. When he first was thrown into this camp, Bettleheim was too weak to swallow food. But an "old prisoner," one who had been there four years, said to him:

> Listen you, make up your mind: do you want to live or do you want to die? If you don't care, don't eat the stuff. But if you want to live, there's only one way: make up your mind to eat whenever and whatever you can, never mind how disgusting. Whenever you have a chance, defecate, so you'll be sure your body works. And whenever you have a minute, don't blabber, read by yourself, or flop down and sleep.

Bettleheim goes on to say, "What was implied was the necessity, for survival, to carve out, against the greatest of odds, some areas of freedom of action and thought, however insignificant." In his book *The Informed Heart* Bettleheim concludes that in the worst of circumstances, the individual must find and hold on to his right to know and act, preserve his "consciousness of freedom," if he is to survive.

I WISH NOW to draw some principles concerning the psychological bases of freedom from this discussion. First, *freedom is a quality of action of the centered self.* We have indicated above that it makes no sense to speak of "part" of the mind or self controlling the rest of the mind. Nor does it make sense to speak, as our Victorian fathers did, of the "will" controlling the mind, or as our Freudian colleagues do, of the "ego" as the seat of freedom and autonomy. David Rapaport has written an essay entitled "The Autonomy of the Ego" as part of the recent developments in Freudianism which seek to include some margin of freedom. Jung has a chapter in one of his books entitled "The Autonomy (or Freedom) of the Unconscious." Or someone might, following Walter B. Cannon's *Wisdom of the Body,* write on "the autonomy of the body." Each has a partial truth; but is not each also fundamentally wrong? For neither the "ego" nor the "unconscious" nor the body can be autonomous or free by itself.

Freedom by its very nature can be located only in the self acting as the totality, the "centered self." [4] Consciousness is the experience of the self acting from its center. The individual's neuromuscular apparatus, his past genetic experience, his dreams, and the infinite host of other more or less deterministic aspects of his experience as a living organism are related in their various ways to this centered act and can only be understood in this relationship.

Certainly one reason for the confusion about freedom in psychology, and a chief reason why psychological studies in the past have confused and covered up rather than revealed the meaning of freedom, is precisely that they have fragmented the person, chopping him up into "stimuli" and "responses" or into "id, ego, superego." We destroy his centeredness by these methods even before we start to study him. If we are to discover anything about psychological freedom in our research, we obviously need some approach like Gordon Allport's "statistics of the single individual," or idiographic method. Or, as I would propose, methods relying on *internal consistency* in the individual and *significant patterning* in contrast to the fragmentation.

The second principle is *freedom always involves social responsibility.* We found in our definition of mind above—the capacity to transcend the immediate situation in time and space and think in long-term consequences—that we could not escape bringing in the social pole of mind. Subjective "mind" and objective "world" are inseparable correlates.

This principle brings in the *limits* of freedom. Freedom is not license nor ever simply "doing as one pleases." Indeed such living by whim or the state of one's digestion is in a sense the exact opposite to the acting of the centered self we have been talking about. Freedom is limited by the fact that the self always exists in a world (a society, culture) and has a dialectical relation to that world. Abram Kardiner has pointed out in his study of Plainville, U.S.A., that the people in this small mid-western town subscribed "in the main to the American credo of vertical mobility and believe that a man can become anything he wants to. Actually opportunities are very limited for them . . . even if they go away." [5] The error in the Plainville credo, as in most of our popularized ideas of freedom, is that they are externalized—they see the self acting on the world, rather than the self existing in a dialectical relationship *with* the world.

A human being's freedom is limited by his body, by illness, by the fact that he dies, by the limits of his intelligence, by social controls, *ad infinitum*. Bettleheim could not change the inhumanity of the concentration camp, but he could become conscious that he was the one enduring these inhumanities; and then already he has partly transcended them. The capacity consciously to confront limits, normal or barbaric as they may be, is already an act of freedom and liberates one to some extent from self-crippling resentment.

Our third principle is *freedom requires the capacity to accept, bear and live constructively with anxiety.* I refer of course to the *normal* anxiety all of us experience at every step in our psychological growth as well as in this upset contemporary world. For some years I have believed that the popular definition of mental health as "freedom from anxiety" is wrong. It has played into the tendencies of the individual to surrender his originality, take on "protective coloring," and conform in the hope of gaining peace of mind. This emphasis on freedom *from* anxiety has actually tended to undermine freedom.

All of us, to be sure, are in favor of freedom from *neurotic* anxiety —the kind which blocks people's awareness and causes them to panic or in other ways to act blindly and destructively. But neurotic anxiety is simply the long-term result of unfaced normal anxiety. When the developing individual, for example, confronts the crisis of weaning, at a later stage the separation from parents in going off to school, then the emergence of sexual problems in the teens, and finds he cannot deal with the anxiety involved but needs to repress it, he has begun the train of events that ultimately results in neurotic anxiety. The same is true with us adults facing the imminence of thermonuclear war: if we repress our normal anxiety in the face of this terrible possibility, we shall develop neurotic anxiety with its various symptoms.

To be free means to face and bear anxiety; to run away from anxiety means automatically to surrender one's freedom. Demagogues throughout history have used the latter strategy—the subjecting of a people to continuous unbearable anxiety—as a method of forcing them to surrender their freedom. The people may then accept virtual slavery in the hope of getting rid of anxiety.

A caution arises here about the use of drugs to reduce anxiety. The use of tranquillizers (except in cases where the patient's anxiety is unbearable, causes destructive regression, or renders him inaccessible to treatment) is highly dubious. We should face the fact that in taking away the person's anxiety, we also take away his opportunity to learn; we take away some of his resources. Anxiety is the sign of inner conflict, and so long as there is conflict, some resolution on a higher level of consciousness is possible. "Anxiety is our best teacher," Kierkegaard said. "He therefore who has learned rightly to be anxious has learned the most important thing."

Freedom is something you grow into. I question the oversimplified statement that we are "born free," except in terms of potentialities. I prefer, rather, to emphasize Goethe's insight in *Faust*, as quoted in the epigraph that heads this chapter.

Let me speak of my own impressionistic picture of the free man. The free man is conscious of his right to have some part in the decisions of his social group or nation which affect him; he actualizes this consciousness by affirming the decisions, or if he disagrees, by registering his protest for the sake of a better decision next time. The free man has respect for rational authority, both that of history and that of his fellowmen who may have beliefs different from his own. The free man is responsible, in that he can think and act for the long-term welfare of the group. He has esteem for himself as an individual of worth and dignity—not the least of the sources of this dignity being his knowing himself to be a free man. He is able, if need be, to stand alone, like Thoreau—willing to be a minority of one when basic principles are at stake. And perhaps most important of all in our day, the free man is able to accept the anxiety which is inevitable in our shaken world and to turn this anxiety to constructive use as motivation toward greater "consciousness of freedom."

I SHALL CLOSE by pointing to how this reexamination of freedom and responsibility affects counseling.

First, we have emphasized that freedom and responsibility always imply each other and can never be separated. Second, our discussion points toward the constructive uses of anxiety, and indirectly toward the constructive uses of guilt and guilt feelings in counseling. Guilt is the subjective experience of our not having fulfilled responsibility, that is, not having lived up to our own potentialities or our potentialities (for example, in love and friendship) in relationships with other persons and groups. Our discussion of freedom indicates, however, that we should not as therapists and counselors transfer *our* guilt and *our* value judgments to the counselee and patient, but endeavor to help him bring out and confront *his* guilt and its implications and meaning for him. Certainly our aim is to relieve *neurotic* guilt feelings, but neurotic guilt is, like neurotic anxiety, the end result of unfaced earlier normal guilt. Permit me to state without here giving the reasons supporting my statement, that the constructive confronting of normal guilt releases in the counselee and patient both his capacities for freedom and his capacities for assuming responsibility.

Third, our discussion points toward the fact that values are presupposed at every point in the counseling process. We need to ponder again the profound meaning of the values that lie in the mere fact of the counseling relationship—the strange situation in which two persons sit down and devote themselves for an hour to the problems of one of them, the counselee. This involves asking again on a deeper level the meaning of what the Germans call *Mitsein* ("being with") and Buber calls the I-Thou relationship.

Fourth, our discussion also points to the fact that values are presupposed in every step the counselee makes in his own integration, but not in the sense that the counselor's values or even society's values are handed over or subtly implied as the only possible ones or the preferred ones. The counselor can best help the counselee arrive at his own values by admitting (though it need not necessarily be verbalized) that he, the counselor, has his own values and has no stake in hiding the fact, but that there is no reason at all to presume that these will be the most meaningful or fitting values for the counselee himself.

NOTES FOR CHAPTER 12

1. See the review by Thomas Szasz of the book *Reality Therapy* by William Glasser, M.D. Dr. Szasz points out that Dr. Glasser relabels everything now called "mental illness" as "irresponsibility." Since, then, the distinction is not made between the moral standards of the patient and those of the therapist, the stage is set for the values of the therapist to be enforced upon the patient at worst, and at best the mores of society to be handed over to the patient under the caption of "adjustment" and "mental health." I understand Dr. Glasser's therapy was worked out originally in his function as psychiatrist in an institution for delinquent girls. This makes sense: the psychopathic personality is the one clinical type which is agreed to be without "conscience" to begin with, and cannot be reached without developing in the patient some social sense. But to extend this type of therapy to every kind of patient is hopelessly to confuse the whole problem of neurosis and mental illness, and to make the therapist society's agent for the destruction of the patient's autonomy, freedom, inner responsibility, and passion.

2. Carl Rogers, "Learning to be Free," paper presented at Conference on Evolutionary Theory and Human Progress: Conference C, The Individual and the Design of Culture, Dec. 2-14, 1960. Mimeographed transcription, pp. 15-16, 79.

3. Carl Rogers has presented empirical studies which demonstrate this point.

4. This concept comes from and is developed in the writing of Paul Tillich.

5. Abram Kardiner, *The Psychological Frontiers of Society,* Columbia University Press, New York, 1945, p. 4.

13

Questions for a Science of Man

In the days when an idea could be silenced by showing that it was contrary to religion, theology was the greatest single source of fallacies. Today, when any human thought can be discredited by branding it as unscientific, the power previously exercised by theology has passed over to science; hence science has become in its turn the greatest single source of error.
—MICHAEL POLANYI, Personal Knowledge

If we are to study and understand man, we need a human model. That sounds like a truism, and it ought to be one; the amazing thing is that it is not a truism at all. I am continually impressed by the surprise registered by our scientific colleagues in other disciplines such as physics and biology when they find us taking our models not only from their sciences, but often from outmoded forms of their science they have already discarded. They are likely to add another truism, "Of course you must have a model which comes from the level of complexity of what you are studying, the human being."

This lack of an adequate model is related to another curious state. That is, despite all the general discussion of psychotherapy and modern man's emotional problems in our scientific journals and the daily press, we still do not have a working science of man on which we can base psychotherapy. I do not presume to offer in this chapter any such worked-out science, but I do entertain the more modest hope that the following remarks will be of help in pointing toward fruitful and basic questions.

By "science of man" I do not mean merely the lumping together of psychology, sociology, anthropology, and the other disciplines which Dilthey called the "cultural sciences" in contrast to the "natural sciences." Certainly these cultural sciences will have much to do with any adequate understanding of man. But by science of man I mean something different, namely, a working theory which will enable us to understand and clarify the specific, distinguishing characteristics of man. It would be the science on which we could base psychotherapy. If the phrase still is ambiguous, as it well may be, I trust it will become clearer and more precise as this discussion proceeds.

It is our lack of such a science that makes possible the great theoretical confusion about the aims of psychotherapy today. Nobody has a very clear idea of what this animal, man, is whom we psychotherapists study and try to help, or even of what help consists in. Indeed, there are indications that contemporaneous psychotherapy is in a peculiar dilemma: at the very moment that it becomes more widespread in its application and training facilities become greater, its inner theoretical confusion becomes more evident. A dozen years ago, for one example, the American Psychoanalytic Association appointed a committee to work out a definition of psychoanalysis. The committee labored industriously for four years, plying the members with questionnaires. But the only point that could be agreed on was a technical one, namely, that analysis was something that should take at least four hours a week. The committee finally had to report back that the theoretical uncertainty was so great that no definition could be arrived at.

I DO NOT propose here to try to enumerate or evaluate the many different kinds of research now going on. I wish only to point out that research tends to follow the lines of the sciences in which clear assumptions and methods are already laid down and for which laboratory equipment is already available. The major share of researches reported in psychiatric journals deal with somatic therapy, according to the study by the Group for the Advancement of Psychiatry.[1] "Next in order of prominence come studies of anatomical, physiological, and biochemical correlates of psychiatric illness. Here the medical background of the psychiatrist, with his many years of focussing upon organ and tissue pathology, dictates research interest." [2] Until recently the study of psychodynamics and psychopathology has constituted only a minor part of the research in psychiatry. Though there is a current trend toward such studies, they will have to be accelerated greatly, this report indicates, to come up to the research into somatic therapies and somatic correlates of psychiatric illness.

The most dramatic and far-reaching progress in the psychiatric field of late, as everyone knows, has been in the development of drugs to control anxiety, depressions, and other forms of emotional disturbance. These drugs obviously have their value with highly disturbed patients to protect them from themselves, to relieve their unbearable anxiety and depression, and to help a much greater number of patients into the state in which they are amenable to psychotherapy.

But the very use of these drugs only throws into more vivid relief the necessity of our arriving at an adequate science of man. The reasons for this are as follows. The drugs for emotional problems work on a very different principle from those which destroy invading germs or viruses in organic illnesses. A number of the drugs block off the painful effects of the emotional state but they have no effect whatever upon its cause; they can change the organism's reactions, but they do not touch the problem of why the reactions are distorted in the first place. A sedative, for example, can help you get a good night's sleep, but it does nothing about the problem which would have kept you from sleeping. It still may be valuable for you to get that sleep, particularly if it fits you on the morrow to attack your problem more effectively. On the other hand, taking the sleeping pill may have aided you precisely in avoiding your problem; it may remove from you the motive for taking some step ahead in your own development. This simple illustration may make clear the not at all simple point that it is in general harmful to patients to take away their symptoms without helping them to cure the underlying problem which causes the symptoms. The function of symptoms in general is to furnish the incentive and direction-finder to get at the underlying trouble. Psychologically, anxiety and depression are nature's way, if we may so speak, of telling the person that he has an underlying problem that requires effort toward correction.

If these drugs for psychological disturbances and the mood-changing drugs now being perfected become widely used, as will almost certainly be the case in the next decades, without equivalent aiding of the persons to solve their problems, we will probably witness the emergence of new kinds of psychological and psychosomatic disorders in our society on even broader scales than at present. Chief among these disorders, if I may venture a prediction, will probably be endemic states of apathy and what I have called elsewhere the experience of inner emptiness.[3] Thus in no sense will these drugs make less urgent our psychological understanding of man; indeed, it will only become the more crucial that we overcome our confusion about the nature of this creature we work with and arrive at some science of man to guide us in our research in psychotherapy.

OUR MODEL FOR a science of man also cannot be taken over lock, stock, and barrel from medicine. Obviously much confused thinking takes place among experts as well as intelligent laymen on the relation of medicine to psychiatric and psychological problems. The essential point which must be seen with clarity is that psychiatric disorders (excluding the minority with an organic basis) and psychological problems have a different character from the diseases which medical methods have treated so successfully during the past decades (e.g., the dramatic success with polio). This was profoundly argued by Harry Stack Sullivan, is passionately argued by Thomas Szasz, and is just argued by many others. The essence of the medical method is the defining of the disease entity, then the isolating of the invading organisms (germs, viruses), and the developing or discovery of the specific drug or vaccine which will destroy those organisms. But as Dr. Stephen Ranson accurately pointed out,[7] while the

> organic medical diseases are predominantly classifiable into relatively discrete disease entities . . . this seems inherently impossible with the case material of psychiatry. The latter seems

instead to consist of reaction patterns or interaction patterns (patterns of living) showing the greatest possible variability. ... [Organic disease consists of] patterns of aberrant phenomena *within individuals*. On the other hand, the functional psychiatric disorders ... refer ... to the interaction of individuals with other individuals, or groups. .... In short, the organic diseases and the psychiatric disorders seem to represent phenomena taking place in different frames of reference.

Dr. Ranson rightly concludes that "extensive review of our basic theoretical structure is in order." The implication is clear, also, that since these disorders occur on a new level of discourse, i.e., the interaction among individuals, and among individuals and groups, a new scientific framework is needed rather than merely an extension of biology or physical science.

Even more striking is the need for a new level of discourse when we pass from psychiatric disorders (such as psychoses) to emotional and psychological problems (typically neurotic and behavioral difficulties). Here the most fascinating and enlightening revelation is to be observed in the struggles in Freud's long pilgrimage to find methods by which he could adequately explore human psychic life. These struggles are described in the letter he wrote to his friend Fliess during those first lonely years of research when practically no one understood or supported his work. Freud, trained of course as a physician and neurologist, explained time and again to Fliess, a physiologist, his endeavors to interpret hysteria and other psychological problems in neurological, organic terms. But each time he was disappointed and found that he had to move on to a new level for his explanations. In one poignant passage written in August 1897 he tells his friend how his great hopes for attaining fame by his theories of hysteria were dashed to the ground, and he adds, "In the general collapse only the psychology has retained its value." He even asks Fliess, plaintively and perhaps ironically, to "give me some solid ground on which I shall be able to give up explaining things psychologically and start finding a firm basis in physiology!"

Freud was a true explorer in that he followed wherever the data led, even though it meant laborious mountain climbing into new ranges where the old charts and methods no longer served. In this sense he had the spirit of the philosopher as well as the scientist. "When I was young," he wrote to Fliess, "the only thing I longed for was philosophical knowledge, and now that I am going over from medicine to psychology I am in the process of attaining it." Indeed, Freud finally had to break with Fliess because the physiologist had "the firm idea of establishing biology on a physical, mathematical formula," but Freud knew that the truths he sought had to be explained on a new level of integration. As Ernest Jones says in his biography of Freud, "We know that the medical study of man's physical afflictions brought him no nearer and perhaps even impeded his progress. That, however, he finally attained his goal, though by an extraordinarily circuitous route, he rightly came to regard as the triumph of his life."

In the science of man certainly medical and other biological data will be highly significant. I wish only to emphasize, however, that we, like Freud, are confronted with something new under the sun of modern science.

The confusion about man, of course, is not the fault of the psychoanalysts, psychiatrists, or psychologists, but cuts like a fissure through our whole culture. We shall see more clearly what we are talking about if we glance back through history for a moment to get our historical bearing. The genius of modern man since the Renaissance has been in the understanding and mastery of physical nature. The methods for this new control of nature were formulated by several philosophers and scientists of the seventeenth century; we shall look at the graphic formulation of Descartes. He held in his *Discourse on Method* that reality has two sides: on one side is matter, that which can be measured, is objective, and has extension—that is to say, physical nature, including the human body. On the other side is thought, mind, that which is subjective and cannot be measured. Descartes and the other philosophers and scientists of the seventeenth century did not mean to split the world in two. Their idea of reason was what Paul Tillich calls "ecstatic"; they were not dualists. Indeed Descartes tried to encompass body and mind by holding that they are connected by the soul which resides in the pineal gland at the base of the brain. Now we know where the pineal gland is. But it has obviously been hard for investigators to find the soul residing therein. Descartes made the typically modern error of trying to define the soul as a thing, an entity.

The upshot of this dichotomy was that modern man then gave himself over with abandon to the pursuit of one side—namely, nature which could be measured. The method now made it possible to place a distance between nature and man and to study nature as objective, something "out there." This approach achieved tremendous success in physics and chemistry, and later in biology and medicine. Understandably, the sciences which best fit the new mathematical methods made the most progress. Understandably, too, these methods that were so magnificently rewarding in the natural sciences were applied to man; the aspects of human experience which seemed to be rational and tangible and could be measured were singled out for study, but the subjective problems—values, consciousness, freedom, responsibility—were put on the shelf as not worthy of study, or were denied outright. By the middle of the nineteenth century, this split between the objective and subjective aspects of life had deepened into a fissure splitting the whole culture as well as the individuals within the culture.[4] The individuals in the late nineteenth century suffered a psychological compartmentalization—which was precisely the disorder Freud sought to cure in his development of psychoanalysis. In its simplest form psychoanalysis is a method for bringing the irrational and rational, the "object" and "subject," back into unity, a method for making man whole again.

Today we know a great deal about bodily chemistry and the control of physical diseases; but we know very little about why people hate, why they cannot love, why they suffer anxiety and guilt, and why they destroy each other. As we stand beneath the fateful shadow of the H-bomb, however, we have become vividly aware that there can be desperate perils in a scientifically one-sided study of nature and man.

Indeed, so much emphasis is placed on the object side of Descartes' dichotomy in our society that the tendency is to assume that it is the only approach. Dr. William Hunt makes this error, in my judgment, when he states in his Salmon lectures: "Psychiatry, and psychology along with it, for the past twenty years has been on a vast psychodynamic splurge to the neglect and sometimes almost to the exclusion of the organic, physiological side of the picture. The pendulum is bound to swing back, and there is evidence that the return swing is beginning." This seems to me to reflect a short-term reading of history. To be sure, Dr. Hunt is right if he is arguing against the superficial psychologizing that has gone on in the recent past. In some circles of Greenwich Village or Park Avenue, you couldn't even get fatigued without someone accusing you of trying to evade responsibility or harboring suppressed resentment against your mother-in-law. Certainly, the sooner we are through with that kind of psychologizing, the better. Let us not for a moment underemphasize the organic aspects of reality and experience; as Kierkegaard would say, nature is still nature, and I would add fatigue is still fatigue. But this does not change the fact that our emphasis has been in modern times overwhelmingly on the organic side; we know a great deal about the physiological aspects of people's behavior but we are still largely illiterate about their psychological, social, and spiritual motives. Our problem is whether we can cut below the split between body and mind and deal with man directly in terms of his distinguishing characteristics as man.

The new emphasis on man's relation to nature and his continuum with animals which has characterized American philosophy and science, including psychology, during the past half-century has been sound in its goal. True, we had broken too much with nature. But I think precisely the reason for this separation between man and nature was the dichotomy we are discussing: the tendency to posit nature and animals as purely objective, "out there." Now it stands to reason that our relation with nature and infrahuman organisms cannot be adequately reestablished by a further overemphasis on one side of the dichotomy. Furthermore, every being must relate to other beings on the basis of its own indigenous characteristics.

As a solution to this problem, many of our colleagues energetically argue that we can avoid the whole difficulty by simply concerning ourselves with behavior. This is the Lockean model—the behavioristic psychologies being what Allport calls the Lockean forms of psychology dominant in England and America.[5] Behaviorism in general avoids the Cartesian dichotomy by redoubled emphasis on one side of it. But the simple fact, which we see demonstrated every moment in psychotherapy, is that people do react to an inner experience of their environment.

When Mr. A comes into my office, for example, I must be sensitive to all aspects of his behavior—his tense eyes, his fugitive smile, his anxious movements, the fact that he sits in an overrelaxed way, lights a cigarette but only takes short puffs from it. These are all data as well as what he tells me about his problems. But his dreams and his phantasies are data too. I must also be aware of how I feel at the time, for I am the part of his world with which he is now trying to communicate. As Niels Bohr puts it, even the modern physicist must be aware that as a scientist he is actor as well as spectator, and I as the therapist am the instrument by which this Mr. A communicates with the world at this particular moment. All of these and hundreds of other data are significant. The chief trouble with behaviorism for us therapists, in short, is that it leaves out so much behavior.

When Bohr, Heisenberg, and other physicists point out that the Copernican view that nature can be separated from man is no longer tenable and that "the ideal of a science which is completely independent of man (i.e., objective) is an illusion," [6] the chief impact on us psychologists, I feel, should be one of liberation. We should see boldly that we have followed too narrow views of science. For example, the method of mathematical quantitative measurement as the ideal for science is a peculiarly modern invention, owing much to the bringing of Arabic numerals into Europe in the late Middle Ages. The basic aim of science from the time of the Greeks down was the discovery of the *lawfulness* of reality. This lawfulness can be demonstrated by methods other than quantification. Internal consistency is one such method; the discovery of patterning is another.

Another shortcoming of behaviorism as a model for a science of man is that it does not take sufficiently into account that man is the mammal who can be aware that he is being conditioned. When the human being is not merely giving himself over to the arbitrary conditions of the laboratory or is not unconscious or under drugs or hypnosis, he can know he is being conditioned, and in this moment he can pause between stimulus and response. This pause, even though it may be only for an instant, enables him to throw some weight toward one response or another. It is thus not accurate to speak of the human being as only the "product" of conditioning. Behaviorism and other forms of experimental and laboratory psychology admittedly have their significant and useful roles, but they must be placed in a broader context of the nature of man and science.

WHAT DOES IT mean to have an emotional, or "mental" problem? Specifically, what is the *locus* of emotional problems? If you look into your own experience you will see immediately that a new category is necessary; the usual terms "body" and "mind" are not enough. It is popularly assumed that body affects mind, and mind body; and if you add the two together you get the person. But this is not at all the whole story, or even the central core of the story. Let us say, to take a simple example, you are fatigued bodily. Now how this will affect your "mind" depends, not on the fatigue itself, but rather on how you, in your self-awareness, relate to the fatigue. If you can accept your fatigue—say it is from skiing or swimming— the fatigue will be pleasant. If, however, your fatigue arises from doing some duty that you didn't like and you fight it, you will probably experience irritation. If, in the third place, you cannot even admit the fatigue to yourself but have to repress it, it will have a different effect: you will probably work compulsively with artificial but unproductive spurts. Here is a simple bodily state, fatigue, that has had three very different effects, depending on how you, in your self-awareness, relate to it.

Again, let us take a so-called mental or emotional state, anxiety, and see how it affects the body. If you are able to accept the anxiety, it will do you no particular harm and may even be an educative opportunity for you. If, however, you resent and fight it, it will have another effect; you may well become depressed, tired. If, in the third place, you cannot accept it, but resort to repression, then it may actually contribute to harmful psychosomatic effects, such as giving your ulcers a flare-up. In each case, we see that it is not just that body affects "mind" or "mind" affects body: rather the crucial question is, *how does the person, in his self-awareness, relate both to body and mind?* The crucial category is the self in its relation to itself.

What shall we call this? Self-awareness? Self-directiveness? Well, some of our psychological colleagues will already be worried: this smells too much like the old idea of "soul." They will remind us, "We could not establish psychology as a science till we got rid of that." This is of course why many psychologists in the behavioristic tradition would also reject the term "self." They hold that these ideas are used to beg the question: "Someone is said to do something because his 'self' or 'soul' causes him to." They are right in the respect that such question-begging obviously is not good science— nor good philosophy or religion, I might add. I have always had the suspicion, however, that it was a defensive science that avoided problems by ruling them out; and that it would be much more in keeping with the scientific mind to try to study the functional meaning of the concepts of "soul" and "self" down through history. Aristotle meant by soul the active, rational principle in man; and he was no fool. I think Descartes, with his crude modern distortion of conceiving of the soul as a thing located at the point where head meets body, was really trying, no matter how unsatisfactorily, to describe the capacity by which a person is able to be aware both of mind and body. One of the aspects of Freud's courage is that he frankly used the term "psyche" and made no bones about it. I am not proposing any of the above as solutions, but I do think we must get over our fear of intellectual ghosts if we are ever to get anywhere. We need to overcome our illusion that things must be concrete to be real, or that only the quantifiable is true, if we are to make progress in the understanding of man and his problems.

I NOW PROPOSE to summarize some elements essential to a science of man. Every science must be applicable to the peculiar, distinguishing characteristics of the subject to be studied, which in our case is the human being. We begin then by asking, what are the distinguishing characteristics of the mammal man?

First, we observe that man is the mammal who talks, who uses symbols as language. Even the chimpanzee brought up with human beings does not learn to talk. Man's ability to use language is based on his capacity to deal with reality symbolically—which is simply a way of disengaging something from what it really is, such as the two sounds which make the word "table," and agreeing among ourselves that these two sounds will stand for a whole class of things. Thus the human being can think and communicate in abstractions like "beauty," "science," "reason," and "goodness." This presupposes the capacity to relate to more than the immediate, given concrete situation and to deal in universals.

Another characteristic we observe is that this mammal, man, keeps time. This is the simple yet marvelous capacity to stand outside the present and to imagine one's self back in yesterday or ahead in the day after tomorrow. A sheep can keep track of time, can "plan for the future," as Howard Liddell puts it, only up to about ten minutes and a dog up to about half an hour. But man is the "time-binding" mammal: he can bring the past of hundreds of years ago into the present and use both past and present in planning for the distant future. Some students of human nature hold that this time-binding capacity is the "essence of 'mind' and 'personality' alike" (Mowrer, Korzybski). It does not make any sense, of course, to say that since the sheep can plan for ten minutes and man for five hundred years, that man simply has this capacity 26,280,000 times greater than the sheep. Obviously a matter of that difference of quantity is also a difference in quality. The chief indication of man's ability to transcend the immediate is his capacity to plan beyond his own death—he can see the world as though he were in it or were not in it.

This is why the human being is the peculiarly historical mammal: he is not merely pushed by his history, like every mammal, but he can be aware that he is pushed and thus can select those aspects of history he wishes especially to participate in and to have influence his development the most. This is the root, furthermore, of his capacity to influence, minutely though it may be, the march of history in his nation and society as a whole.

A further characteristic we observe in the subject before us is his peculiar capacity for social interaction with his fellows. You may say, "This is not unique: many organisms are 'social.' Take ant colonies and flocks of sheep." To be sure, but the ant colonies, intricately organized as they are, have not varied for five thousand years. I owe to Howard Liddell the statement that the so-called gregariousness of the sheep "consists of keeping the visual environment constant." Only at two periods, mating and suckling, does the sheep interact with other sheep in terms of their nature as sheep; at other times the "flock" can consist of collie dogs or children, providing it is constant. But the human being becomes—or at least can become—aware of his interpersonal relationships; he opens himself to the influence of certain persons and more or less rejects others. He is thus able within a margin to mold and modify his relationships with his fellows; he is, in his self-awareness, partially the author of his society and the giver of meaning. A group of individual animals makes a flock; a group of human beings makes a community.

We pause now to ask, what is the common denominator of these three examples we have cited? In the first chapter we have identified this as man's capacity to transcend the immediate, concrete situation and to experience himself as both object and subject at the same moment. I mean this not at all intellectualistically or detachedly— he *experiences* himself as object and subject, which means he relates to both these poles with feeling, with some value judgment, and greater or lesser commitment. He can think of himself *as* the person who needs to act in a given situation as well as at the same moment *being* that person. As you read this page you are the *object* of my words. But at the same time you can be aware of yourself as a *person who* reads the words, that is, the subject. And you thus have some margin of freedom to decide how much you agree or disagree.

This unique capacity to transcend the concrete situation has, according to the late neurobiologist Kurt Goldstein, its neurological corollary. The frontal cortex is known to be the part of the brain that is very large in human beings, but minute or almost nonexistent in lower animals. Goldstein showed that when the frontal cortex of the brain is injured, patients lose precisely the capacities we have been talking about. They are always occupied with concrete matters like where their clothes are placed; they write their names, when given a sheet of paper for the purpose, not somewhere in the center of the paper but in the very corner where the immediate, concrete boundaries orient them. They cannot transcend the immediate and the present, Goldstein indicates, and they progressively lose the capacity for abstract thinking.

Obviously man's ability to see himself simultaneously as subject and object is very close to what is often termed "self-relatedness." But self-relatedness in this context I am suggesting implies the capacity to relate to other selves as well as to one's own self. It is to be radically distinguished from egocentricity. We know through the work of Sullivan and others that lack of or distorted awareness of one's self blocks one's awareness of others; and the more clarified one's capacity is to see himself as subject, the more he can know other selves.

Furthermore, this being subject and object at the same time underlies our peculiar awareness of the world around us. If the truth were known, this is the capacity by virtue of which we can *be scientists* in relation to nature: that is, we can think of nature "out there," can temporarily separate subject and object, and can think in abstract, universal laws with respect to nature. Indeed, the most extreme behaviorist who insists on treating nature and human nature with "pure objectivity" and is scandalized by the concept of "self" is able to assume his objective attitude toward nature only by virtue of his own capacity for self-relatedness.

At this point we need to point out that the phrase "man in his environment" is inadequate. Every organism has an environment, to be sure. But a unique relationship occurs between human beings and their environment. As the highly suggestive research in perception and projection indicates, men view and interact with the environment in terms of their own symbols and meanings, and some of the character of the environment for them depends upon these symbols and meanings. When we realize how much individual projection, normal as well as distorted, takes place, let us say, in Jones's relation to his environment, and how freighted with special meanings that environment is for Jones, we see how inaccurate it is to speak of the environment as though it could be described as something apart from Jones. I often feel that the behaviorists and others who assume an objectively real environment do not take seriously enough the fact that logically (as demonstrated not only in philosophy but in modern physics) their assumption is an imaginative construct, useful for the particular abstract scientific purposes of the moment but not possessed of reality in itself.

In any case, this is why we in these chapters speak of the self as having a "world" rather than an environment. Self-relatedness presupposes the existence of a structured world in relation to the self; the specific form of the general "organism-environment" category applied to human beings is "self-world."

We now confront the question, how is self-relatedness, this capacity to experience one's self as subject and object, different from what is called self-awareness? Self-awareness is the conscious, intellectual aspect of self-relatedness. But it is not the whole of it. Indeed, there is a real danger in some schools of psychotherapy that self-relatedness may become too intellectual, too verbalistic, something talked about rather than lived. This error is especially to be warned against inasmuch as some readers may interpret my phrase "transcending" as meaning living in an ivory tower, above day-to-day concrete realities, cushioned in the new scientific womb of blissful abstractions. This is a radical misunderstanding.

For self-relatedness includes subconscious levels as well as conscious awareness. When you commit yourself to love, for example, or to some other form of passion or to a fight or to an ideal, you ought to be, if you are to be successful in your love or fight, related to yourself on many different levels at once. True, conscious awareness is present in your commitment; but also you experience subconscious and even unconscious powers in yourself. This self-relatedness is present in self-chosen abandon; it means acting as a whole; it is the experience of "I throw myself into this."

The technical term for this experience of abandon is an old one which I propose we see in a new meaning—namely, ecstasy. A word with roots *exstasis,* literally meaning "standing out from," ecstasy is present in all creative activity. The opposite kind of abandon is the state of panic or being spellbound. Both ecstasy, at one pole, and panic and being spellbound at the other, involve acting as a whole person; but note how great the difference! In panic and the state of being spellbound, self-relatedness is at a minimum: the person acts blindly, irrationally, without free choice. And the newspapers say, "He acted like an animal"—which is an unfortunate insult to our infrahuman relatives. But ecstasy is not irrational, it is trans-rational. Anyone who has ever really made love or painted or seriously been in a fight or experienced creative ideas knows that ecstasy brings a *heightened* awareness; one gets ideas he didn't know he had; one's vision may be improved, one can see more keenly what to do, can vary his actions, and a sharpness of reason and judgment wells up as it were from subconscious levels. Self-relatedness, as we illustrate in ecstasy, is more than conscious, intellectual awareness.

This brings us to a remark about self-relatedness and the body. When Nietzsche said, "We think with our bodies," he did not mean that thought is a physiological process. He meant that the body must be included in any complete relatedness to one's self. One of the aspects of modern man's loss of relatedness to himself is that his body gets caught in the subject-object split: he tends to regard his body purely as an object, something external, to be studied chemically, to be calculated and controlled. The body is seen like the rest of nature in the Newtonian sense, something to get power *over*. Assumptions of this sort, for example, are present in the Kinsey methods, that people can be considered as sexual "objects" and that sex can be studied statistically apart from its subjective, interpersonal meaning. Persons who come for therapy with these attitudes generally reveal a considerable isolation from the body. Nietzsche was wiser than many of our modern scientific assumptions. The body is one aspect of the self: it is one form of our intercommunication with the world, and as such is an integral part of self-relatedness.

A SCIENCE OF MAN must have as its fulcrum the unique, distinguishing characteristic of man, namely, his capacity to relate to himself as subject and object at once. Let us now ask how such a framework would be of aid as a basis for our understanding and research in psychotherapy.

We see immediately that the subject-object concept gives us a guide in our research into the developmental origin of the special processes in the human being that lead to psychological and emotional problems. For example, we know that the capacity of the little infant to use language and symbols, his vulnerability to neurosis, and his self-relatedness develop simultaneously as different sides of the same process. Lawrence Kubie accurately wrote:

> the neurotic process arises with the development of language in infancy and early childhood, that is, with the development of the capacity to act and think and ultimately to speak in symbols. The symbols of neurosis parallel the symbols of language and depend upon many of the same fundamental human capacities; and the neurotic distortion of these symbolic functions occurs as a result of a dichotomy between conscious and unconscious processes which starts early in the development of each human infant.[8]

In fact, this very split between consciousness and unconsciousness occurs chiefly because the infant is blocked in developing his capacity to see himself as subject and object. What the infant can communicate to his parents becomes "conscious," and what he cannot communicate (because of anxiety or fear of punishment) gets blocked off, repressed, made "unconscious." This is why Kierkegaard very rightly said, "The more consciousness, the more self."

This framework gives us, furthermore, a perspective in which to gauge neurosis and psychosis. The blocking off of self-relatedness is what Freud called "repression" and Sullivan termed "dissociation."

The degree of this truncation of self-relatedness is a measure of the neurotic development in the person. Complete lack of self-relatedness is present, of course, only in psychosis. Our neurotic problems thus occur in proportion to how much we have been forced to surrender our capacity to see ourselves as subjects and objects at the same time. Psychological freedom is acting in accord with one's own character.

We come here to a very ticklish question. Because of man's capacity to see himself as from the outside, to relate to himself as subject and object at once, he can act *against* himself. As Paul Tillich puts it, "In nature action follows being: cats act according to 'cat being'; they do not act against the essence of cat. But man can act against his own nature; we thus have in language the category of 'unhuman.'" I suspect that much behavior that is called tragic in human experience, much of what Freud meant by the "death instinct," is to be understood in the light of this potentiality of man for acting against the self.

These considerations indicate why an adequate science of man also cannot exclude ethics. For the actions of a living, self-aware human being are never automatic, but involve some weighing of consequences, some potentiality for good or ill. Again, in proportion to the absence of self-relatedness—say when the person is under drugs, hypnotized, or suffers from severe neurosis or psychosis— this weighing of consequences is proportionately less. Ethics arise from man's ability to transcend the immediate, concrete situation and to view his acts in the light of the long-run welfare or destruction of himself and the community.

The outlines of a science of man we suggest will deal with man as the symbol-maker, the reasoner, the historical mammal who can participate in his community and who possesses the potentiality of freedom and ethical action. The pursuit of this science will take no less rigorous thought and wholehearted discipline than the pursuit of experimental and natural science at their best, but it will place the scientific enterprise in a broader context. Perhaps it will again be possible to study man scientifically and still see him whole.

NOTES FOR CHAPTER 13

1. *Collaborative Research in Psychopathology*, formulated by the Committee on Psychopathology of the Group for the Advancement of Psychiatry, Topeka, Kansas, January 1954.
2. *Ibid.*, p. 3.
3. May, *Man's Search for Himself*. Since the writing of the original paper on which this chapter is based, there has been a good deal of evidence that the prediction above has come true, namely, that apathy has appeared in our society, and threatens to become endemic, if it has not already become so. The case of the murder of Catherine Genovese, with the thirty-eight citizens of Queens refusing to get "involved," is only the most dramatic of incidents which indicate this apathy.
4. See Ernst Cassirer, *An Essay on Man*; and Rollo May, *The Meaning of Anxiety*.
5. Gordon Allport, *Becoming: Basic Considerations for a Psychology of Personality*.
6. Quotation from a mimeographed address by Werner Heisenberg at Conference on Science and Human Responsibility, Washington University, St. Louis, October 1954.
7. In a paper delivered at the 1954 annual meeting of the American Psychiatric Association.
8. Lawrence Kubie, *Practical and Theoretical Aspects of Psychoanalysis*, 1950, p. xiii.

14

Social Responsibilities of Psychologists

*The moral man is not the one who merely wants to
do what is right and does it, nor the man without
guilt, but he who is conscious of what he is doing.*
—HEGEL *(1770-1831)*

This topic challenges us not only because of its importance to us
as social scientists, but also as human beings living in a precarious
period of our world. During the days when I was first working on
the essay on which this chapter is based, the President had just
announced that there was one slim chance still open of getting a
test ban, failing which the genie of thermonuclear war power and
its companion devil, overkill, would be out of the bottle for good.
Those same days the news was full of reports of the hundreds
imprisoned in Birmingham. And the very evening I was writing
down some of these ideas, a riot occurred in Harlem and a march
down Amsterdam Avenue in New York City, past Columbia
University and half a block from our home. A couplet from
Shakespeare's last four lines in King Lear kept running through
my mind,

"The weight of this sad time we must obey,
Speak what we feel, not what we ought to say."

If we then had the illusion that as soon as those two problems
quieted down, we should be relieved of our precarious state, we were
disillusioned soon enough. For we soon saw our marines land in the
Dominican Republic, with the result that a "permanently precarious"
state is insured, and since then the war has escalated in Vietnam—

for which, no matter what one's political views, there seems no ultimate outcome which is not negative. I mention these things to indicate that there seems little doubt but that we shall be in a precarious world situation for some decades to come: unless we blind ourselves to the realities, we shall live "in crisis" for a good while. It therefore behooves us the more as psychologists to be concerned with the question of social responsibility.

The first thing that strikes us as we consider this topic is that we as psychologists, until four or five years ago, did not take our social responsibility in any adequate way or to the degree our society has a right to expect from us. In 1954 Arthur Compton called a conference on Science and Human Responsibility. It was, I fear, indicative of our detachment that there was only one psychologist present. The conference was made up of physicists, like Compton and Heisenberg, biologists, philosophers, and humanists. Nuclear physicists in particular have been way ahead of us in taking responsibility on the overriding issue in our world, namely, thermonuclear war. Fortunately the situation has changed in the last several years: psychologists have taken their place in the front ranks on these issues. I think there is this difference from the physicists: the psychologists have taken their part as responsible citizens, and so far as I can see, what is still lacking is a responsible concern with the fact that the development of the science of psychology itself contains dangers to the society, just as did the development of physics.

Why was it that the nuclear physicists committed themselves a number of years before psychologists? Not because they alone knew the tremendous destructive power of nuclear weapons: we all knew that after Hiroshima. Their own hands had had a part in making the bomb, and their social detachment was irrevocably shaken. Can their commitment and responsible concern not be rightly interpreted as a constructive reaction to their own guilt? One of the physicists remarked at the time of the first fission, "Not one of us walked away from that look-out point at Los Alamos without saying to himself, 'God! What have we done?'" Not that any serious number of them believed that they should not have developed the atomic fission that made the bomb possible—that would have meant a scientific turning back which, even if it were possible, is unthinkable from their point of view or ours. But the shaking of their self-world relationship which they directly experienced fortunately did result among many of them in the emergence of a new level of consciousness, a level which now perforce was to include social responsibility.

I propose, similarly, that a constructive facing of our own guilt as psychologists is our healthiest place to start. This may well sound strange in most psychology departments, where at the most it would be admitted that this guilt is only potential, not actual. But it would be a pity indeed if we had to wait, as a profession, until some such cataclysmic change in the mind and spirit of modern man forced us to wake up to the power we are playing with. Robert Oppenheimer has already reminded us, in his speech before the American Psychological Association convention in 1955, that the psychologist's responsibility is even greater than the physicist's. "The psychologist can hardly do anything," said Oppenheimer, "without realizing that for him the acquisition of knowledge opens up the most terrifying prospects of controlling what people do and how they think and how they behave and how they feel." [1]

If Oppenheimer's words are correct—and to me it seems obvious that they are—the logic of our situation requires that we strip away professional trappings and make a more profound and searching self-examination than we or any profession is used to. Perhaps it is fitting that a psychoanalyst take the role of Socrates' gadfly in submitting some queries for such a self-examination.

THE FIRST QUERY is our tendency to rationalize lack of commitment by the rubric "wait-till-all-the-evidence-is-in." But are not the critical situation of our contemporaneous world and the nature of the issues precisely such that they cannot wait for critical tests? We cannot wait for a test of thermonuclear war; we cannot wait for a full test of radiation. The irony of our situation is that if we wait for all the evidence, we shall not be here to use the evidence when it comes. My argument, of course, is not at all against the disciplined endeavor to gain all the evidence we can. It is, rather, against the use of this respectable ideal as a substitute for commitment. As though if we waited around long enough, the evidence would make our decisions for us! Robert Lifton well remarks in his study of thought control, any complete "personal or moral detachment in psychological (or any other) work is at best self-deception, and at worst a source of harmful distortion." [2]

But an even more important point for us as psychologists in this connection seems to me to be this: that the nature of the issues we face is such that *we cannot know the truth except as we commit ourselves*. In Chapter 2 we mentioned the statement of a participant in a debate on the issues of nuclear war, addressed to the people listening, "You cannot have any influence whatever on the question of whether there will be war or not. This is decided by the councils of the few high political men who gather in Berlin or Moscow." My answer was, "I admit what you say *seems* to be true, and you have plenty of evidence for it. But even if you had all the evidence in the world, I still would not believe it."

As the audience well realized, I was not making an anti-intellectual statement. I was saying, rather, that if we accepted my opponent's statement, we would remain passive; and the statement would become true by virtue of our accepting it. If, on the other hand, we refused to accept it, but did what little we could to influence Congress, the President, and other leaders, then even a group as small as several hundred would have some significance.

This is the point where political freedom begins, infinitesimally small as it may be to begin with. And it is the faith of democracy that such influence can increase geometrically like a benevolent chain reaction. We all know that democracy can deteriorate into a blind faith in quantities and numbers and gross statistics. But is not democracy in its origins, and in its highest representatives, something quite else, namely, a faith in a *quality of personal commitment?* By the same token, is not freedom not at all a matter of "doing as you please," but rather the power of one's actions as a person to have significance, to *matter,* to his group?

My point is that the critical experiences of life, such as love, war, and peace, cannot come into being until we commit ourselves to them. And statements about these experiences cannot be true except as we, or somebody, commit ourselves responsibly to the beliefs. We shall return to this question in our discussion of values below.

A SECOND QUESTION that arises in such a self-examination is our *naiveté about the problem of power.* As I observe psychologists, I find us sharing in abundant measure that aspect of the vocational disease of the Western intellectuals—the failure to see, indeed playing ostrich with, the tragic, demonic aspects of power. In the earlier studies of race relations, I failed to see in the work of psychologists an awareness of the explosions in desegregation and in race relations that were to occur.[3] Did we not underestimate the degree of explosive power of the accumulated repressed passion (in a Freudian sense) and the pressure of economic determinants in the suppressed group (in a Marxian sense)? The artists, in the persons of novelists like Lillian Smith and James Baldwin, turned out to be better predictors of the turmoil and rioting in desegregation than we were.

The basic problem here is that our frame of mind as psychologists seems to be one which denies and represses power. As I see it, we tend—again sharing in that symptom of the vocational illness of Western intellectuals, overemphasizing rationality—to take literally Aristotle's dictum that man is a rational animal because it makes our hypotheses simpler, permits us the comfort of continuing as mild-mannered men who assume that other men act as rationally as we *think we* do. And since our tests are set up on our own presuppositions which overlook or deny power, they naturally come up with results which fail to reveal the power needs which drive people or groups.

I have often thought, as I have interviewed psychologists for analytic schools, that there is a selective factor at work in that our profession tends to attract the type of individual who denies and represses his own power needs. These repressed power needs then have room to come out in his proclivities for controlling other people in therapy or in his identification with the power of his laboratory techniques and machines. In candidates wanting to be trained as therapists, I see not infrequently the pattern of the isolated person who wants relationship and gets attracted into doing therapy because it gives a simulated relationship which makes him feel less isolated—a "captive" love affair or friendship, which of course is no love or friendship at all, and a failure of therapy, to the extent that it is captive. Similarly, the unexpressed and unfaced power needs of psychologists going into research find a made-to-order form in which to find expression, namely, preoccupation with the power of techniques to control others.

One aspect of self-deception in connection with the above is that our belief that the pen is mightier than the sword tends to slip over into an unexamined assumption that therefore the sword, or power, is irrelevant. And *mirabile dictu,* we then fail to see that the spoken or written word can be as irresponsible and as vicious as the sword. When someone attacks you with the sword or attacks you economically as in Madison Avenue business competition, you at least can see what you're up against; whereas words which are used for power purposes, as in thought control, can be more vicious and harder to withstand in the respect that they attack the center of identity and self-consciousness.[4]

The less we play ostrich with the problem of destructive power, the more we can effectively help ourselves and our society shift our power needs toward positive goals. Take, for example, the problem of peace. In my college days, we believed in peace, marched for it, campaigned for it, and were so conditioned to "think peace" that we never let a thought enter our minds that there might be another war. But this made us totally unprepared to see or deal with Hitler; we did not even *perceive* this emergence of evil power (for a length of time I am ashamed to remember) because such irrational, primitive power just did not fit our categories and concepts. It simply could not exist. But it *did* exist, whether we could let ourselves see it or not. The liberal intellectuals of Germany and Europe fell into the same trap; they played into the hands of the dictators because of their failure to take the tragic realities of power into account, and they thus consequently failed to commit themselves in time.

What I am advocating—as a hoped-for consequence of this self-examination—is a widening and deepening of our consciousness to take in the problem of power in its tragic, dynamic, and demonic aspects. If I were teaching a course in beginning psychology, I would assign some reading of Karl Marx, not for the sake of his economic philosophy, but because he understood the basic significance of irrational economic and social power, and he saw how the way you get your power conditions the particular set of "rational" beliefs ("ideology") you choose. It is possible thus to reconstitute our consciousness in wider dimensions to include perceiving and understanding the socially destructive aspects of power, and also to enlist our own aggression and power needs on the constructive side of social issues. Is this not what William James sought as the "moral equivalent of war"? Peace will then not be a vacuum—a passive, zestless, unheroic and boring state—but will challenge and require our full potentialities.

A THIRD QUESTION for self-examination is the antihistorical tendency in psychology. We are prone to see ourselves as "above" history and to fail to see that our psychology, and indeed modern science itself, are historical products like any other aspect of culture. Science has taken several quite different forms in Western culture; and it is surely arrogance to assume that our own is the absolute and final form of science. The Greek view, that science is the uncovering of *logos,* a meaningful structure of the universe, was based upon the Greek's special respect for nature. The medieval view, formulated by the scholastics and Aquinas, that all nature fits together into a rational order, became the basis for modern experimental science; it gave scientists the faith that all the segments of their diverse research could fit together and make sense. In modern times *power over* nature rather than uncovering and understanding became the goal (vide Bacon's dictum, "Knowledge is power"). And methods of attaining power were to be based on the model of the machine. Thus began the preoccupation of Western man with the calculation and control of physical nature.

Two developments, then, have been fateful for our dilemma as psychologists in our contemporary world. One was the shifting, in the seventeenth century and subsequently, of the moral absolutism and authority of the church to science. The second was the endeavor, beginning in the nineteenth century, to make *man also* an object of calculation and control, and to apply the methods which were still so impressively productive in gaining power over physical nature to gaining power over human beings.

Precisely here, it seems to me, lies the dilemma of modern psychology. We are the representatives of modern science who are ordained to function in the realm of man's mind and spirit. (And the dilemma surely cannot be escaped by our substituting other terms like "behavior" and "awareness.") We are heirs, whether we are conscious of it or not, to the mantle of moral absolutism of science, and the mantle weighs upon us (like Hercules' shirt) more precariously than upon the physicists, who deal with inanimate nature, or the physicians, who can at least tell themselves they deal with the body. We are handed by society, whether we wish it or not, the requirement of producing answers to the ultimate questions of ethics and the spirit; and it is expected in many quarters, both outside scientific fields and inside, that we shall produce these answers by our techniques and our machines. Our dilemma, then, is whether we can have a science of man and at the same time avoid the tendency to make man over into the image of the machines and techniques by which we study him. That is, whether we can have a science of psychology and still preserve the values and distinguishing characteristics which make man a person, the values that constitute his humanity.

There are no easy answers to these questions; but I believe there *are* answers; and many of us would not be in the field of psychology at all if we believed there were not. The question above, then, is not *whether* but *in what way* can we have a science of man and preserve these values?

Society, of course, harbors a good deal of ambivalence toward psychology. This is sharper and more radical than the usual ambivalence toward science. We are expected to play God, but are feared and hated as the devil in the same proportion as we are worshiped. The playing of God on the part of a state or a science or a group of persons will inevitably result in this God-creature being seen as the devil.[5] But it is indeed a tempting prospect—good authority tells us the most powerful and deadly temptation of all.[6] It is at this point that our examining of ourselves is crucial. And can we not find useful assistance for this self-examination, unpleasant though such assistance always is, in the criticisms of our profession made in our society?

I refer to the "riots" in the Long Island community against educational testing; to such books as *The Brain-Watchers;* to the criticisms of William S. Whyte of vocational testing and psychotherapy; to the attack of Joseph Wood Krutch on Skinner's operant conditioning. It seems to me that our tendency to think ourselves "above history" has blinded us to the underlying meaning of these criticisms, let alone helping us to cope with them constructively. Do we not largely miss the point if we simply call those attacks "unfair" and dismiss them by proving the authors wrong in their factual details? The problem is not that one cantankerous individual writes a book or that some vociferous groups or individuals are victims of misapplied tests or certain vocal individuals are casualties of therapy. No; it is much more fruitful and accurate to view these attacks as symptomatic of an underlying distrust of us in our society coming to the surface. We should ask, symptomatic of what kind of distrust, and for what reasons? Certainly William Whyte and Joseph Wood Krutch, to cite only two examples, cannot be thought of as unenlightened or obscurantist or undevoted to the public welfare.

Surely the first query to ourselves is, *Have* we indeed tried to play God? There is nothing so unexpected in this query. Speaking of the relation of contemporary tendencies to deify science and thought control, Robert Lifton has these cogent words to say:

> Accompanying this deification is the expectation that science will supply a complete and absolutely mechanistic theory of a closed and totally predictable universe. Modern physics has

long disowned this ideal, but it persists in the human sciences—biological, psychological, and social—and is particularly damaging there. Thought reform is its ultimate expression—a mechanized image of man within a closed society, and a claim to scientific method in the remaking of man in this image.[7]

I have pointed out in the preceding chapter how we have fallen, in my judgment, into the role of playing God in psychology. What implications does the situation have for the problem of our social responsibility?

SOME OF OUR colleagues hold that the accepting of our social responsibility requires our taking on the role of controlling and manipulating others. I do not agree, not only because such a course goes against my democratic view of society, but more important, because I believe that course works against the emergence and development of human values. Not that any of us denies for a moment that human beings can be controlled within certain limits and for a certain period of time—by drugs, by conditioning, by hypnosis, and by thought control. Nor can any of us deny that some element of control and the setting of conditions is present in all human relationships—therapist with patient, parent with child, teacher with student. But the critical difference is made by whether this control presupposes the other person as *subject* or *object;* whether or not the control is associated with manipulation—strictly speaking, the "use of the hands (*manus*)" in molding another—or for the purpose of enlarging the other person's consciousness and freedom to participate responsibly in the choice of social values?

Some examples of what we mean by control may be of interest. For one example, I teach my child, firmly and with genuine control, to wait for the green light when crossing the street. But I am not trying simply to establish a new habit, inculcate a new form of behavior. I try to open up to him the principle, explain the situation, with the hope that, as he grows, his consciousness will be enlarged to take in "traffic" aspects of experience that can then help him adapt to future situations which I know nothing about, traffic on new superhighways or (heaven help us) traffic someday among the stars. In this sense, the control from me is in the service of enlarging his conscious responsibility and margin of freedom.

Take also an example from therapy. We are all entirely aware how much control goes on in therapy. But to the extent that it is control in the service of molding the patient into a given way of behavior, I believe it is the failure of therapy rather than the success. Certainly, the therapist rightly has much to do with setting the conditions of therapy, in accord with the reality facts of time and space; e.g., there are certain hours set aside for the patient; he does not come any time he pleases or to any place he wishes. But the important point is not centrally that the patient *fit* these conditions. Rather, *how* the patient reacts to the conditions, questions them, defies them, etc., is most important of all when we see as the central purpose of therapy not inculcating new habits, but providing a situation in which the patient's sense of identity, significance, and responsibility may be discovered and developed.

A patient of mine, for example, came consistently late to his sessions. I could easily enough condition him out of this obviously self-defeating "bad habit." But it was much more important for me to join with him in trying to see what he was saying in his coming late (telling himself as well as me, since he is not aware of why he comes late and therefore does not have as yet responsible control over it). For this particular patient, whose whole previous life had been in the context of a powerful and famous father, coming late was in the early stages of therapy a constructive, independent act. Indeed, it would be a distinct loss if he got over the symptom before he had the chance to understand the language of the symptom and hear what it was telling him. I am most dubious of all about the patient who fits our "conditions" too well—the compliant patient, who seeks to please and who tries to ferret out what he thinks I believe he should do and then is only too anxious to do it. We get *apparent* successes with this kind of patient (success that may last over several years), but in the long run I believe prognosis for this type is most dubious of all. It is significant, in this respect, that studies of conditioning therapy indicate that the patients who are most compliant, susceptible to hypnosis, suggestible, are the ones most responsive to the conditioning type of therapy.[8]

Our problem consists, then, of understanding the nature of social values and the interrelationship of the individual's freedom to those values. In my judgment, our fulfilling our social responsibility in the positive sense will depend on how we as psychologists solve this problem of the relation of individual freedom to social values.

I propose that *there is a dialectical relationship between social values and individual freedom, and that we cannot have one without the other*. In human civilized cultures, there is no such thing as a purely *social* value as such; values are given and transmitted in the tradition of the society and are constantly subject to affirmation, development, and re-forming by individuals in the society exercising some margin of freedom to affirm or defy. These values emerge continuously on new levels of consciousness as the individual interacts with his group. If we have only something that can be handed over by the culture, irrespective of the conscious choice or affirmation of the individual, we have *mores, customs*. I am using the term "value" to indicate a pushing forward toward some new form of behavior—goals, ends of life to which we are devoted and toward which we choose to move because we believe them to be more desired ways of life. This dialectical relationship between individual freedom and social value is established both in the subjective consciousness of the individual and in his objective behavior, and changes society as it goes along.

Some twenty years ago I argued in several papers that values were necessary and inevitable in the aspects of psychology and psychiatry which had to do with helping people—namely, psychotherapy. This point of view was pretty generally rejected then, but is fairly broadly accepted now. But the conclusion that therefore the psychologist should prescribe values to others was no better a solution. It shows a grossly oversimplified view of values. There is a tendency among therapists to reflect the ethos of the particular historical period in which they live. Thus they prescribe the values of their own group to patients who, out of their own anxiety and confusion, are clutching at some way of life that gives security—and therapists of course can inculcate the values of their group with techniques of psychological influence parallel to brainwashing. Though this indeed may make for "adjustment" and some kind of temporary security and "happiness," it works against ethical sensitivity and creativity and against the emergence of the new which, I contend, is a necessary part of any viable value.

It is important to keep the point clear that though our science may test certain values, the *content* of the value itself does not come from science. We can set up research into people's attitudes and ways of communication on peace, and the relation of these attitudes to security or panic, but the belief in peace itself must come from something more than our science. The fact that leading German doctors, including Jewish doctors, worked for Hitler in his program of extermination, makes it clear that expert training in science is not enough to insure a humanitarian choice of values. Heisenberg, in charge of the National Institute of Physics in Nazi Germany, decided to work to keep Hitler from getting the atom bomb not because of his science but because of his humanity.[9]

The content of values comes by and large from religion, philosophy, and other disciplines in the humanities; and this is as it should be. If science does not give the content of the values, this is not because science has not progressed far enough as yet. It is, rather because the content of values and the testing which science does are on two different levels. As Albert Einstein put it, the scientific method

> can teach us nothing else beyond how facts are related to, and conditioned by, each other; . . . the aspiration toward such objective knowledge belongs to the highest of which man is capable. . . . Yet it is equally clear that knowledge of what *is* does not open the door directly to what *should be*. . . . To make clear these fundamental ends and valuations, and to set them fast in the emotional life of the individual, seems to me precisely the most important function which religion has to perform in the social life of man.[10]

We not only do science a disservice when we expect it to do everything, including furnishing our values; we also block ourselves off from several thousand years of slowly evolved human wisdom and render ourselves naive in relation to values.

I WISH FINALLY to bring out several considerations with respect to the interrelation of individual freedom and social values which I believe are essential to a solution of our problem.

The first is that *the emergence of a new value occurs to a greater or lesser extent as an attack upon the existing values of the society.* The new value is in one sense a "resistance to acculturation" as Maslow puts it, indeed a temporary breaking of acculturation. This attack upon the culture occurs both in the conceiving of the new value and in its application. One has only to look cursorily at our Western tradition or any tradition to see that ethical leaders, like Socrates and Jesus, were considered such enemies of society that they were executed by the state. They certainly *were* enemies of the state as *status quo.* Their being rewarded by the society by execution is as we would expect: for the *status quo* must be opposed in order that there may emerge some new value which is essential to the growth and ethical awareness of the civilization. This is what Tillich means by "the god beyond god."

The second consideration has to do with the importance of preserving and respecting *the individual's right and capacity to question.* One principle all the systems of manipulatory control have in common is that the individual cannot question the basic assumptions. A very important and rich source of data here is Lifton's study to which we have already referred. He describes the impressive and amazingly intelligent system of rewards and punishments the Chinese communists devised for reeducating their prisoners by the methods of thought control. If you, as prisoner, could accept the framework, you could get on fairly well. But the fundamental point was, *you must not question the ultimate assumptions on which the system is based.* The basic goals are set by someone else, in this case the communist hierarchy, with no relation whatever to this given individual; he is entirely the object of techniques.

But the capacity to question basic goals is one of the characteristics which distinguish man as man in the evolutionary scale. And is not the questioning of goals such as the war system, even national sovereignty, our one chance of taking a responsible hand in the directing of our own evolution? [11] My own experience is chiefly on the level of the psychotherapist, working with human beings in intense anxiety and profound suffering, in some cases on the brink of psychosis—levels, that is, when the usual pretenses of life are thrown aside. I am convinced by more data practically every hour of the day that the patient's emerging capacity to question the goals, let us say, which exploitative parents imposed upon him, or his own sado-masochistic goals, is a highly significant point in his movement toward health. This principle seems obviously true beyond the area of neurosis or psychosis.

To be able to question is the beginning of one's experience of identity. The function of questioning is that it distinguishes self from world, makes possible the experiencing of one's self as a subject in a world of objects. The danger, when a person is treated as an object of control and fundamental questioning is prohibited, is that this experiencing of the self as a subject in relation to a world of objects is lost.

THE THIRD consideration in our understanding of the relationship between individual freedom and social values is perhaps the most important of all. It is that *human values are never a simple one-way street, but always involve a "no" as well as a "yes"*—what I shall call here a *polarity of will.* Indeed, is not every event in human experience a dialectical relation between such positive and negative poles? The reason the right to protest, to cast a negative vote, has been so precious in Western history as an earnest of the dignity of the person, from the time of Amos and Micah down through the Areopagus in Athens, the Magna Charta in England and so on, is that this negative will actually constitutes, that is, makes possible, the positive will. I have stated above that the capacity to question is the beginning of the experience of identity. I state now that this freedom to say "no" is what gives *substance and power* to one's experience of identity, in that it proves that what one feels and thinks *matters.* And this makes the possibility of being a rebel,[12] of experiencing anger and engaging in revolt, potentially constructive experiences.

In psychotherapy we must, of course, deal with this polarity of reaction all the time, and I often think it is the most critical point in the question of whether we can help another person to health. Freud saw this, and met the issue in his emphasis on bringing out the hostility and negative transference of the patient. Rank described it specifically as the polarity of will and based his whole system of therapy upon it. Jung described it in pointing out that a negative element will always be present in consciousness on any question as a counterbalance to the positive element and in rough proportion to it. I believe, by the same token, that one of the weaknesses of Carl Rogers' system of therapy is his underplaying of the negative aspect of will. For example, in the practice of "congruence" I find a tendency to cover over the emotional differences between patient and therapist, to limit the variety and depth of affects dealt with in therapy, to underestimate anger, hostility, and conflict. The patient experiences his identity standing *against* as well as with the therapist, and covering over the negative elements makes this harder for the patient. Rogers has, of course, been in the forefront of those insisting on respect for the patient. But is not respect best and most profoundly shown by openly admitting anger, hostility, and conflict with another, but at the same time not withdrawing one whit from the relationship? Indeed, such "inclusion of the negative" normally can make a relationship, and the mutual respect in it, more solid and trustworthy.

This negative-positive element is obvious in physical nature, in the attraction and repulsion patterns of neutrons and protons; but it assumes much greater significance on the level of human consciousness. For me to be "conscious" means I can be aware of the fact that *I* am the one rebelling, denying, experiencing hostility or anger; and I therefore can and in principle to some extent must take some responsibility for it. This follows as a datum of psychological experience: to be conscious of the fact that it is one's own anger, rebellion, etc., already constitutes an element of responsibility. The fact that the exceptions to this are pathological (e.g., the defiance of the psychopath) only demonstrates the point the more. Consciousness consists of figure-ground—to think one thing I must at the moment exclude other things; to perceive one thing, I must shut out, "deny," all other things for the instant. In this sense, *conflict is of the essence of consciousness.*

The polarity of will I am speaking about may not come out much as yet in our laboratory, empirical studies, but this should not surprise us. For our presuppositions, the very context of our thinking, tend to rule it out to start with, and consequently it does not appear in the results. There are a number of significant bodies of data to study, however.[13] Take, for example, Dollard's studies of the situation of the American Negroes. The white man has been rewarding acquiescent and punishing rebellious behavior for a long time, and in the South he assumed he was getting some kind of adaptation from the Negro. But appearances are very deceiving: what he actually got, as Dollard showed, was apathy, indifference, laziness, and apparent stupidity as a defense against the white man's pressures. These symptoms may be rightly looked upon as neurotic protests, camouflaged rebellion of the Negro to preserve a pseudo-identity in a situation of inability to rebel outright. We are now reaping the deeper reaction which was repressed under these symptoms, namely, resentment, anger, passion for revenge.

This has far-reaching implications in psychology and certainly in psychotherapy. In work with people where we seem to get agreement without this negative element being in some degree present, we may really be getting simply conformism, apathy, lack of zest, and indifference.

My point that the element of rebellion is built into the structure of human consciousness, and is one of the elements which constitute consciousness, is given emphatic support in classical myths, which are the repository in quintessential form of human experience over many centuries. The myth of Prometheus, for example, presents the ancient Greek conviction that culture itself, including its values, is born in a rebellion against the gods.

It is interesting that both B. F. Skinner and his erstwhile debating opponent Carl Rogers underestimate the significance of human conflict. (Is the reason for this omission that they both, like good enlightened Western psychologists, overestimate the rational aspects of man and underestimate the irrational?) We recall in our first chapter Skinner's describing as sheer nonsense Dostoevsky's argument that "men will prove they are still men and not the keys of a piano" by revolting against the controller out of sheer "cussedness." Can it not be that Dostoevsky is picturing ironically the normal, healthy tendency in man to rebel against overreaching authority, as Adam did long ago in Eden, as Prometheus did in archaic Greece, as the English nobles did against King John, as the Hungarians did against the Russians, as the present-day younger poets in Russia do against the regime that would "do them good," and prefer to risk imprisonment rather than accept what others believe is good for them? Could it not be that Dostoevsky is speaking of the same trait in man that another Russian, this time a great poet, Alexander Blok, referred to when he made a speech on the occasion of the eighty-fourth anniversary of Pushkin's death? In this oration in 1921, "The Poet's Destination," Blok described the "freedom and tranquillity" that contemporary Russian authorities were taking away from the poet—

> Not outward but creative tranquillity. Not
> the childish do-as-you-will, not the freedom
> to play the liberal, but the creative will—
> the secret freedom. And the poet is dying,
> because there is no longer anything to breathe;
> life has lost its meaning for him.[14]

I am aware that I also beg the question by citing examples from Russia, which might be rebutted as obviously examples of "inept control." But I don't think that changes the issue. The rebellion of Adam and Prometheus in the myths was not against wholly inept authorities, but expressed positive goals in the development of human civilization and consciousness.

If you want a fairly exact picture in contemporary psychology of a modern Garden of Eden, you have only to read Professor Skinner's *Walden Two*. In *Walden Two* there is freedom from anxiety, guilt, and conflict; you are good and wise without trying or choosing to be, and like Adam and Eve under the trees, personal relationships are "under the most favorable conditions," as Professor Skinner phrases it. Under the benevolent dictator of *Walden Two,* the people are said to be happy. But it is a post-human, animal happiness, with the capacity to question and constructive dissatisfactions lost. Though I disagree with *Walden Two,* I am not worried about it, for all that I know about human beings as a therapist or as a student of human history leads me to be confident that if there were a next chapter in the book, it would be a resounding revolt against the dictator and the system; and whether the dictator is malevolent or beneficent is irrelevant.

If we now look at the myth of Adam as the writers of Genesis presented it, we find its truth is quite different. It is not by accident that this classic myth portraying the birth of human consciousness is a myth of revolt against God. Under the "benevolent dictatorship" of God, Adam and Eve exist in the Garden of Eden in a state of naive, prehuman happiness, a contentment without anxiety, shame, or conflict, and also, like the infant in the first months of life, without moral or individual consciousness. Adam and Eve then go through steps parallel to those I have cited earlier in this chapter. They *question* authority (the question projected on the serpent), they experience *moral consciousness* (partaking of the tree of the knowledge of good and evil). The price they pay for their revolt against the authority of God is shame, guilt, anxiety, conflict, and ejection from the blissful, infant state of Eden. As they set out,

> The World was all before them, where to choose
> Their place of rest, and Providence their guide.
> They hand in hand with wandering steps and slow
> Through Eden took their solitarie way.[15]

But what do they gain as they bid goodbye to Eden? They gain differentiation of themselves as persons, the beginnings of identity, the possibility of passion and human creativity. And in place of the naive, nonresponsible dependencies of infancy, there is now the possibility of loving *by choice,* relating to one's fellowmen because one wants to, and hence with responsibility. The myth of Adam is, as Hegel put it, a "fall upward." It is, indeed, the emergence of human consciousness.

Throughout this book I have been emphasizing valuing as an *act*. This implies an open, rather than a closed, system. We have said above that there is no value except as someone commits himself to it—this also emphasized value as an act. *It is in the act of valuing that consciousness and behavior become united.* One can take over rote values (more accurately called "mores," "standards") from the church, or the therapist, school, American Legion, or any other group in the culture. But the act of valuing, in contrast, involves a commitment on the part of the individual which goes beyond the "rote" or automatic situation. This, in turn, implies some conscious choice and responsibility. The goal assumed throughout this book, deepening and widening of consciousness, is also an open rather than a closed goal, and infuses and informs the open society.

NOTES FOR CHAPTER 14

1. Robert Oppenheimer, "Analogy in Science," *American Psychologist,* Vol. 2, pp. 127-135 (1956).
2. Robert J. Lifton, *Thought Control and the Psychology of Totalism: A Study of "Brainwashing" in China,* Norton, New York, 1961, p. viii.
3. Kenneth Clark has pointed out this problem of power, in race relations, and the challenge it poses for psychological and psychoanalytic theory. Cf. *Dark Ghetto, A Study in Powerlessness,* New York, 1965.
4. Cf. Lifton's study (cited above), to which I shall return.
5. Cf. Lifton, *op. cit.,* p. 502, n. 35.
6. A great wealth of mythological and religious data has this point: cf. Lucifer in Milton; Jesus' temptations in the Gospels, etc. It seems man is in the difficult position of having to revolt against God (as we shall indicate in a later section) without succumbing to the belief that he has the power of God.
7. *Ibid.,* p. 459.
8. Cf. Krasner, *The Therapist as Social Reinforcement Machine.*
9. Personal communication.
10. I owe this quotation to Robert Lifton, *op. cit.,* p. 460.
11. Anne Roe, in her paper, "Man's Forgotten Weapon," *American Psychologist,* 1949, 14: 261-266, points out that the capacity for awareness of one's own and one's society's attitudes—what I call in this paper "consciousness"—is what distinguishes man in the evolu-

tionary scale, and the use of it our one way of exercising a margin of freedom in molding our own evolution.

12. Cf. the positive way in which Camus and other writers have used this experience of being a rebel.

13. See also *The Informed Heart,* by Bruno Bettleheim, to which we have referred above, which gives Bettleheim's highly significant discussion of the "ultimate freedom" of the prisoner in the concentration camp to choose his own attitude in relation to his captors. This preserving of the *inner* right to revolt, even in these ultimate situations in which external revolt was not possible at all, made it possible in many cases for the person to survive. On a more basic level it was a central element in preventing psychological apathy, indifference, and despair (in which states he tended to wither away and die off). And on what to me is the most basic level of all, this inner capacity to choose his own attitude—to reserve the right inwardly to say "no" even though he had to do the specific thing he was ordered to do—is what preserved the person's dignity as a human being. The data in books like Bettleheim's seem to me exceedingly relevant and important. Similar data are given in Victor Frankel, *From Death-Camp to Existentialism,* and Christopher Burney, *Solitary Confinement.*

14. George Reavey, *The Poetry of Yevgeny Yevtushenko,* New York, 1965, p. viii.

15. The quotation is the last four lines of Milton's *Paradise Lost.*